Battleground Europe

CASSEL AND HAZEBROUCK 1940

Battleground Europe

CASSEL AND HAZEBROUCK 1940

France and Flanders Campaign

Jerry Murland

Pen & Sword
MILITARY

First published in Great Britain in 2017 by
PEN & SWORD MILITARY
an imprint of
Pen and Sword Books Ltd
47 Church Street
Barnsley
South Yorkshire S70 2AS

Copyright © Jerry Murland, 2017

ISBN 978 1 47385 265 5

The right of Jerry Murland to be identified as the author of this work has been
asserted by him in accordance with the Copyright, Designs and Patents Act 1988.

A CIP record for this book is available from the British Library.

All rights reserved. No part of this book may be reproduced or transmitted in
any form or by any means, electronic or mechanical including photocopying,
recording or by any information storage and retrieval system, without permission
from the Publisher in writing.

Printed and bound in England by
CPI Group (UK) Ltd, Croydon, CR0 4YY

Pen & Sword Books Ltd incorporates the imprints of Pen & Sword Archaeology,
Atlas, Aviation, Battleground, Discovery, Family History, History, Maritime,
Military, Naval, Politics, Railways, Select, Social History, Transport, True Crime,
and Claymore Press, Frontline Books, Leo Cooper, Praetorian Press, Remember
When, Seaforth Publishing and Wharncliffe.

For a complete list of Pen and Sword titles please contact
Pen and Sword Books Limited
47 Church Street, Barnsley, South Yorkshire, S70 2AS, England
E-mail: enquiries@pen-and-sword.co.uk
Website: www.pen-and-sword.co.uk

CONTENT

List of Maps

Series Editor's Introduction

This is the second in the Battleground Europe series of books on the France and Flanders Campaign of 1940 by Jerry Murland.

In the popular mind – or at least the popular British mind – there are only a few aspects of the 1940 campaign on continental Europe that stand out: the notion of Blitzkrieg, the evacuation from Dunkirk and the odd stirring speech by Winston Churchill. Details over and above that are hazy in the extreme, none more so than the series of rearguard battles and actions that the British Expeditionary Force was forced to undertake as resistance in Belgium collapsed and as German forces (largely mechanised) made the potentially very risky thrust through the Ardennes to the Somme estuary in an effort to further divide the northern allied armies from those in the south.

These books, concentrating as they do on particular locations, do not overly concern themselves with the wider picture of the campaign. However, a few general observations are worth making. There were fundamental weaknesses at the highest levels, political and military, in France and a distinct lack of will. Despite having some first rate equipment, it is difficult to draw any other conclusion than that the French were poorly led.

The British fought with an army that had been systematically under-resourced for too long for the deficit to be made up by a couple of years of frantic rearmament. Political direction had been, to put it at its most charitable, indecisive – at least until Churchill came along. Although the British, once more, were the junior partners in a continental campaign, it is all too easy to point the finger of blame at French senior commanders when there was indecision, poor communication and lack of drive on the British side.

Once it was clear that the Belgian army's defences had been out manoeuvred by bold German action, the allied forces that had been pushed into Belgium under the French Plans D (the Dyle Plan) had not much option but to withdraw or run the risk of being enveloped by the German armoured thrust to the south. To be fair to Lord Gort, commander of the BEF, he had not been enthused about the decision to move into Belgium from the prepared positions that had been occupied since the autumn of 1939.

On 19 May, within days of the opening of the audacious German offensive on 10 May, Gort was given the desperate news by General Bilotte that there were no French troops between the advancing Germans and the sea. Gort made the decision, therefore, that evacuation was the only solution and brought back as many of his troops as possible to a length of sandy beaches, with Dunkirk to the north. On 20th May the planning for Operation Dynamo began; indeed, in reality, the evacuation began almost immediately. There was a final attempt at a co-ordinated action with the French to reconnect with the French forces to the south of the Somme; but this had to be abandoned by the 25th.

It is with this background that the holding actions – for that is what they were – at Cassel and Hazebrouck were fought. By the time that they began, in fact, the evacuation was in practice well under way, with the first large scale evacuation taking place on the 26th. The story of the fighting at the front from the allied perspective is of units and, in some cases, large formations (such as the French holding out in Lille) fighting under considerable disadvantages: poor communications, contradictory orders (or very vague one), without air support, restricted supply of rations and munitions – and so the list goes on.

The units of the BEF that were involved in the area around Hazebrouck and Cassel likely fought with no great expectation of being able to make a successful, cohesive withdrawal when the time came, as it seemed inevitable that it would. It would be optimistic to say that they made any great impact on the German advance; but they did fight capably and their combined efforts along the rapidly changing front helped to slow down the Germans to the extent that a substantial body of men were evacuated, far bigger than might have been reasonably anticipated. This was no great victory, of course - the men might have escaped to England but their precious equipment did not; nevertheless, the sacrifice of units such as 2/Glosters and 1/4th Ox and Bucks at least enabled the extent of the evacuation and the consequent important boost to the sagging morale of the British in what proved to be a pretty awful year.

Cassel and Hazebrouck are set in some rather uninspiring countryside, although Cassel has plenty of charm as an old hill top town where all around is flat. The casualties of the fighting are scattered around in communal cemeteries and cemeteries established by the then IWGC from the previous conflict. When visiting the area some thirty years ago for my first book, I spent time at Wormhout, in the shadow of Cassel a few miles to the south, on the trail of the hideous crime committed against, amongst others, 2/Warwicks by troops of the SS. One of the striking things that I noticed, there and in many other cemeteries where casualties of the 1940 fighting are buried, was the lack of precision about the date of death, with it often being placed within dates sometimes weeks apart. What uncertainty and consequent emotional pain this must have brought to so many relatives back at home.

The founding principle of the Battleground Europe series was to explain events on a particular part of the battlefield, supplemented by unit and personal accounts and relating them, where possible, to surviving features on the ground. In the case of the 1940 campaign there are few of these physical relics; but the landscape is largely unaltered and some places – in this case Cassel – have changed but little. The memory is maintained by the occasional memorial and by graves of the men who fell. I am – and I am sure many others will be – indebted to Jerry for making a visit in the trail of these men of 1940 so much more meaningful.

Nigel Cave
Andover, November 2016.

Author's Introduction

A little over five miles to the northwest of Hazebrouck is the small and ancient town of Cassel. Built on top of a hill, which rises nearly 600 feet above sea level, it dominates the surrounding flat Flanders countryside. Half a mile to the east of Cassel is the wooded Mont des Récollets, standing some sixty feet lower and separated from the town by a shallow valley through which runs the modern day D916. In May 1940 this small hilltop town, together with the larger urban sprawl of Hazebrouck, became two of the lynchpins in the 48th Division's web of defence that held and protected the western face of the so-called Dunkerque Corridor. Created by Lord Gort, the British Commander-in-Chief, the 'corridor' was the escape route through which the bulk of the British forces were able to reach the evacuation beaches on the coast.

Today, a line of canalized waterways, running south from Gravelines through Aire-sur-la-Lys towards Béthune, mark the western edge of the *Pays de Flandre*, while to the east, the A25 Autoroute from Dunkerque runs almost parallel with the Belgian border as it sweeps majestically south-east through Armentières and on to Lille. Now part of the greater *Nord-Pas de Calais,* the region, which Charles

Cassel rises 600 feet above the Flanders Plain

de Gaulle called 'a fatal avenue through which invading armies repeatedly passed', has been has been one of the most fought over provinces in Europe.

Early History

Making an annual appearance every Easter, two legendary giants – Reuze-Papa and Reuze Maman – are said to have created the hills at Cassel and Mont des Récollets when they tripped and deposited two huge piles of earth that they were carrying. These giants make their first appearance on Carnival Sunday, before Shrove Tuesday, and again on Easter Monday. Early records suggest the hill was occupied during the late Iron Age when it was probably the site of a hill fort. The town takes its name from the Roman development of the area when Cassel – renamed *Castellum Menapiorum* - was absorbed into the Roman province of Gallia Belgica in 29 BC. After the collapse of the Roman Empire, Cassel and the surrounding land of Flanders passed into the hands of Baldwin 'Iron Arm', who became the first Count of Flanders in 864 AD. The town was destroyed by the Vikings in the late 9th century and rebuilt by Baldwin's grandson, Arnulf I, in the 10th century. Two generations later in 1071, Arnulf III was killed during the First Battle of Cassel by forces allied to Robert the Friesian who fortified the hill and added a new set of walls built on the old Roman foundations. Although these wall are long gone, the pattern of streets and pathways in the town date back to this period.

In 1328 the Second Battle of Cassel was fought between Philip V of France and Nicolaas Zannekin, who commanded a rebel force intent on seizing Flanders. Zannekin's defeat led to a period of relative calm but by the end of the 16th century Cassel's position as a border town between France and the Spanish Netherlands saw both sides struggling for control of the town. In 1677 the Third Battle of Cassel took place to the west of the town, near Zuytpeene. This was

The memorial on the D138 commemorating the Third Battle of Cassel in 1677

a decisive victory for the French who defeated Dutch forces commanded by William II of Orange and absorbed much of the surrounding area into France. Today, the occasion is sometimes known as the Battle of the Peene and an obelisk memorial stands on the D138 between Noordpeene and Zuytpeene to commemorate the battle.

It was during the French Revolutionary Wars that Frederick, the 'Grand Old Duke' of York and Albany, was said to have marched 10,000 men up the hill. However, it should be said that the nursery rhyme originated well before the Revolutionary Wars and the link with Cassel must be regarded as dubious to say the least!

One of the more well known residents of Cassel was Dominique-Joseph Vandamme, who commanded Napoleon's III Corps at Waterloo in

Dominique-Joseph Vandamme

1815. Granted permission to return from exile in 1819, he died in his native Cassel at his château – which is now in ruins - on the Rue Bollaert le Gavrain in 1829. The town memorial to Vandamme stands at the junction of Avenue Achille Samyn (D933) and Rue de Watten (D11). In 1848 the railway from Lille to Dunkerque was constructed, incorporating a new railway station for Cassel built at Bavinchove with a connecting tram service to the town. In 1934 this was replaced by a bus service, which still operates today.

Hazebrouck

The commemoration of legendary giants is also a feature of the Hazebrouck cultural calendar, when the town's four giants are paraded. Rowland appears in the middle of Lent and again with his family during the first weekend in July. Twinned with the market town of Faversham in Kent, Hazebrouck can trace its beginnings back to the reign of Dagobert I, who cleared the area of forest in 630 AD, but it was not until 1122 that Charles the Good gave the town the name of *Hasbruc*. Like Cassel, Hazebrouck was subjected to the ravages of wars, not only at the hands of Philip VI of France, who burned the town in 1347, but between the Spanish Netherlands and France in their struggle for territory. Hazebrouck was finally annexed by Louis XIV of France in 1678.

It was the arrival of the railway that was largely responsible for the development

The modern town of Hazebrouck, looking north towards St-Sylvestre-Cappel. The photograph shows clearly the open nature of the town's approaches compared to the hilltop fortifications of Cassel. The Church of Notre Dame, which was destroyed during the war and rebuilt in 1959, can be seen in the centre of the photograph.

of Hazebrouck from a small market town to an important railway junction, circumstances which undoubtedly contributed to the expansion of the weaving and spinning industry in the 1860s.

The First World War

Cassel remained behind Allied lines in the war years of 1914-1918 and served as the military headquarters of Maréchal Ferdinand Foch between October 1914 and May 1915. His offices were on the first floor of the Hôtel de la Noble Cour, also known as Landshuys, in the Grand Place, a building which is now the Departmental Museum of Flanders. During his stay at Cassel he lived in the Hôtel de Schoebeque – then a private house - on Rue du Maréchal Foch where a memorial plaque on the wall, to the left of the street entrance, commemorates his links with the building. Foch was a frequent visitor to the Collégiale Notre-Dame de la Crypte near the Porte de Dunkerque; inside is a plaque commemorating his son and son-in-law who were lost in one of the early battles of the First World War. *Aspirant* Germain Foch and *Capitane* Paul Bécourt were killed during the Battle of the Frontiers in August 1914. A monument to Foch, which was unveiled in July 1928 by President Pointcaré, stands behind the windmill on the highest point in the town; a replica of which can be found in Grosvenor Gardens, near Victoria Station in London. The French returned to Cassel in November 1917.

The British moved to Cassel in 1916 under General Sir Herbert Plumer, who established his Second Army Headquarters at the Castel Yvonne in the Rue St Nicholas. The small square in which the 2/Gloucesters established their HQ in May 1940 was originally named in honour of General Plumer, but was changed more recently to honour Dominique-Joseph Vandamme; accordingly I have referred to the square in the text as Place du Général Vandamme.

Field Marshal Haig was a frequent visitor to Cassel and also used the Hôtel de Schoebeque as his residence when in the vicinity. The war artist William Orpen is closely associated with Cassel and amongst his many paintings is one of Plumer, which was painted in the Casino. Orpen also painted the *Household Brigade Passing to the Ypres Salient, Cassel*, in which he depicts the Porte d'Aire. His well-known painting of the courtyard at the Hôtel du Sauvage – now a restaurant – is a reminder of the popularity of the hotel which, Orpen tells us, was packed almost every night with officers from the Ypres Salient who were escaping the rigours of trench warfare 'to eat, drink, play the piano and sing, forgetting their misery and discomfort for the moment'. The painting is now kept at the Imperial War Museum in London.

Douglas Haig commanded the BEF during the First World War

Both Hazebrouck and Cassel felt the weight of the German Spring Offensive in 1918 when Operation Georgette was launched with the aim of capturing Hazebrouck and its railway marshalling yards to cut the supply routes to the BEF. The offensive opened on 9 April and two days later the forward units of the German Sixth Army were less than five miles from Hazebrouck, prompting Haig to issue his famous 'backs to the wall' order. Fortunately, the offensive lost its momentum and the arrival of much needed reinforcements brought the German advance to a halt. But it had been a close run thing, and the number of CWGC Cemeteries that dot the surrounding landscape must have served as a constant reminder to the men of 1940 that the area had already been fought over in 1918 by their fathers and uncles twenty-two years earlier.

Although Cassel has changed relatively little over the years, in May 1940 Hazebrouck was considerably smaller than the modern town of today, which has seen residential and industrial development extending the town boundaries well beyond those of seventy-six years ago. Consequently, most of the positions occupied by the 1/Buckinghamshire Battalion (1/Bucks) during May 1940 have now vanished under the tide of expansion, and the inevitable post 1945 urban improvements that accompanied the town as it rebuilt itself as a road and rail junction. However, despite this, it is still possible to locate the approximate

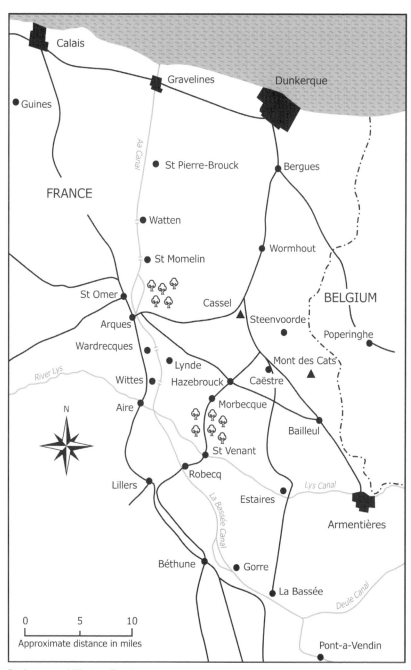

Dunkerque and Western Flanders

positions of several of the Buckinghamshire platoons and the location of Battalion HQ in the centre of town.

The German attack on Hazebrouck was initially from the west but, unlike Cassel, which benefitted from high ground, the openness of Hazebrouck was highlighted by the relative ease with which the German armoured units penetrated the town. An ease which, in retrospect, leads to the question: would the 1/Bucks' defence of Hazebrouck have been more effective if Major Heyworth had reduced his perimeter and concentrated on exploiting the vulnerability of armoured fighting vehicles (AFVs) in urban areas? The narrow streets in Hazebrouck were well suited to this form of warfare, where the limited range of the battalion's anti-tank weapons may well have been employed to greater effect. Certainly they were at an immediate disadvantage when the superior fire power and mobility of the 8th Panzer Division surrounded, and began to systematically overwhelm, company positions on the outskirts of town. However, it must be said that it is doubtful whether the 1/Bucks would have been familiar with this type of defence or, indeed, were in a position to carry it out.

By nightfall on 27 May, effective resistance at Hazebrouck had been crushed by the 8th Panzer Division, leaving only Battalion HQ isolated in the centre of town until the survivors surrendered during the evening of 28 May. At Cassel, the fighting units stood their ground until the orders to withdraw finally arrived on 29 May, by which time they, too, were surrounded, in their case, by units of the 6th Panzer Division.

Information concerning the deployment of the units at Cassel has focused on the detailed descriptions left by Captains Eric Jones, Bill Wilson and others of the 2nd Battalion Gloucestershire Regiment; detail which, rather frustratingly, is lacking in accounts left by the officers and men of the 4th Oxford and Buckinghamshire Light Infantry (4/Ox and Bucks). In fact, the platoon positions of the 4/Ox and Bucks are only generally referred to as being in the eastern half of the town, although careful reading of the accounts of those who were there at the time, do provide an approximate location for each company.

Fortunately, the Defence of Hazebrouck is focussed on a single infantry battalion and the battalion war diary offers a reasonably complete record of what happened. The historian is also fortunate in that the war diary of 98/Field Regiment provides another account of the fighting in and around the town. Moreover, there are several other accounts written by other officers and men who were there at the time, which help to give an overall picture of what took place.

In Appendix 1 the reader will find notes on many of the individuals mentioned in the text, including the senior German officers. Many of the British officers and men were killed or captured during the breakout and their final resting places are noted, along with those who were captured. The ranks given to each individual are those that were held in May 1940.

When describing the fighting I have often referred to modern day road numbering in order to give the reader using current maps of the area a more precise location. While some of the abbreviations in the text are self explanatory, others do require a modicum of explanation. I have used a form of abbreviation when describing units and formations, thus after its first mention in the text the 2nd Battalion Gloucestershire Regiment becomes the 2/Gloucesters or more simply the Gloucesters. German army units are a little more complex. Within the infantry regiment there were three battalions – each one approximately the size of a British battalion – and, as with their British counterparts, the battalion was broken down into four companies of riflemen, who were given an Arabic numeral, for example, 3 *Kompanie*. Again, I have abbreviated when describing these units, thus Infantry Regiment 162 becomes IR162 while the second battalion within that regiment is abbreviated to II/IR162; or, in the case of panzer regiments, II/Pz10. In the same way, Artillery Regiment 76 is abbreviated to AR 76 and German Infantry Divisions are referred to in their abbreviated form, hence the 31st Infantry Division becomes ID31. Equivalent German and British ranks referred to in the text are as follows:

Lieutenant General	*Generaloberst* and *General der Panzertruppe*
Major General	*Generalmajor*
Colonel	*Oberst*
Lieutenant Colonel	*Oberstleutnant*
Major	*Major*
Captain	*Hauptmann*
Lieutenant	*Oberleutnant*
Second Lieutenant	*Leutnant*
Corporal	*Unteroffizier*
Lance Corporal	*Gefreiter*

Acknowledgements

It is always a pleasure to return to this tiny corner of France, where practically every visit is marked by a new insight into the often bloody nature of the history surrounding the towns and villages that dot the landscape. During these visits I have frequently been accompanied by Tom Waterer, Dave Rowland and Paul Webster, who seemingly never tire of wandering around the May 1940 battleground. To them I must offer my thanks for their patience in not only allowing me to follow up obscure references that have been found on maps drawn at the time, or referred to in soldier's accounts, but for being dragged across fields and along obscure pathways in the quest for that elusive piece of evidence. I should add that their input into the various car and walking tours has been invaluable.

I am also indebted to Stephen Berridge, the webmaster of the excellent *Lightbobs* Website, who has answered a number of my queries regarding the Buckinghamshire Battalion at Hazebrouck, as has Ingram Murray, who kindly allowed me to quote from his paper on the 1/Buckinghams at Hazebrouck. My thanks must also go to Dominique Billiet, who is the present owner of the rebuilt Villa de Moulins at Cassel, which D Company of the 2/Gloucesters temporarily occupied in May 1940. His invitation to visit his house and have lunch with him was both a delightful and informative occasion. I also met his charming tenants, Peter and Sandra Floyd, who live in the gatehouse and joined us for lunch.

I was also interested to read Richard McNab's account of his father's retreat to Dunkirk and that he had passed through Cassel and Hazebrouck several times prior to the battle. Major George McNab's impressions of the early bombing of Cassel are included with Richard's permission.

My thanks must also go to the sound department at the Imperial War Museum, the National Archives at Kew and the curators and keepers of records at the Soldiers of Oxfordshire Museum, the West Sussex Records Office and the National Army Museum. In particular I owe Laura Dimmock-Jones at the RUSI Library in Whitehall my gratitude for assisting me in locating obscure volumes buried in the depths of one of the best military libraries in the country. Finally, I am indebted to the WW2 Talk forum, whose members have answered my queries and assisted me in numerous other ways. In particular, Andy Newsom has been very helpful in sharing his knowledge of Cassel.

Chapter 1

Invasion

On 10 May 1940 Germany invaded France and the low countries of Holland, Belgium and Luxembourg. The attack involved three Army Groups advancing simultaneously: Army Group B, under *Generaloberst* Fedor von Bock, advanced through north eastern Belgium; a panzer assault, led by *Generaloberst* Gerd von Runstedt's Army Group A, which attacked through the Ardennes to cross the Meuse with the intention of cutting through the British and French armies. The third group, Army Group C under *Generaloberst* Wilhelm Ritter von Leeb, was tasked with breaking through the Maginot line. Dubbed 'the Matador's Cloak' by Basil Liddell Hart, the German plan was masterly in its simplicity and adopted the code word *Fall Gelb*.

Generaloberst Gerd von Runstedt commanded Army Group A

Up until 10 May Allied forces, under the overall command of

The Phoney War was an eight-month period during which there were no major military land operations undertaken by Allied forces.

General Maurice Gamelin, had concentrated on extending the Maginot Line along the Belgian border, a period of some eight months that became known as the Phoney War. Gamelin's plan to counter the German invasion was for French and British forces to cross the border into Belgium and occupy the line of the River Dyle, which runs roughly north and south about thirty miles east of Brussels. Given the operational code name Plan D, the British Expeditionary Force (BEF) were to deploy between Louvain and Wavre, with the French First Army, under General Georges Blanchard, on their right in the Gembloux Gap. The Belgians, who were expected to hold their positions for several days, would then fall back into the gap between the left of the BEF and the right of the General Henri Giraud's Seventh Army, who were to link up with the Dutch via Breda.

General Maurice Gamelin

It was a plan that certainly puzzled many in the BEF, who had spent the whole of the previous winter preparing defences behind the Belgian frontier. Now, as soon as Germany invaded Belgium, all that was to be abandoned and the enemy was to be brought to battle from positions that were unfamiliar and where the defences were already thought to be of a poor quality. If that was not bad enough, there was considerable doubt over the fighting quality of the Belgian forces and their ability to put up a stout resistance.

General Georges Blanchard

The BEF command structure

In overall command of the BEF was 53-year-old Lord Gort. As a highly decorated Grenadier Guards' officer, he had served in the First World War with some distinction; wounded on four occasions, he had been decorated with the Military Cross (MC) and the Distinguished Service Order (DSO) and two bars. His award of the coveted Victoria Cross (VC) came whilst he was commanding the 1st Battalion during the battle on the Canal du Nord in 1918.

Commanding I Corps was General Sir John Dill, an individual who had served with distinction under

General Henri Giraud

Douglas Haig and succeeded General Edmund Ironside as Chief of the Imperial General Staff (CIGS) on 27 May 1940. After Dill's recall, command of I Corps was passed to Lieutenant General Michael Barker. In command of II Corps was the energetic and able Lieutenant General Alan Brooke, a gunner who rose from lieutenant to lieutenant colonel over the four years of the First World War. Brooke was unconvinced of the Allied chances of holding the forthcoming German offensive, an observation that was not held by Gort, who regarded Brooke as too much of a pessimist. Both Brooke and Dill had drawn Gort's attention to the potential weaknesses of an advance

John Vereker, 6th Viscount Gort, Commander-in-Chief of the BEF

General Sir John Dill commanded I Corps until he succeeded General Edmund Ironside as CIGS in May 1940

into Belgium, views that were seemingly dismissed by the commander-in-chief. By the end of 1939, a third regular division had been formed – the 5th Division – and in January 1940 the first of the territorial divisions arrived, leading to to the formation of III Corps under the command of Lieutenant General Sir Ronald Adam.

The Dyle Line

Operation David, the code word transmitted to every British Army unit on the Franco-Belgian border, signalled the end of the Phoney War and the move east to the River Dyle. The main

Lieutenant General Alan Brooke

fighting force was headed by motorcycle units of the 4/Royal Northumberland Fusiliers and the Morris CS9 Armoured Cars of the 12th Lancers; and was carried out with little interference from enemy activity by the troop carrying companies of the Royal Army Service Corps (RASC). Gort's plan was to place the 1st and 2nd Divisions on the right flank and the 3rd Division on the left astride Louvain. By way of reserve, the 48th (South Midland) Division was ordered to move east of Brussels and the 4th and 50th (Northumbrian) Divisions to the south. In addition the 44th (Home Counties) Division was under orders to march to the Escaut south

The 12th Lancers were equipped with the CS9 Armoured Car. Seen here is a vehicle of C Squadron undergoing a minor service.

of Oudenaarde and the 42nd (East Lancashire) Division placed on readiness to take up station to their right if required.

Events on the Meuse

The campaign was essentially lost on 14 May when German panzer units of Army Group A stormed across the Meuse and headed for the channel ports. This was the so-called 'Sickle Cut' through the Ardennes, which reached the Channel coast on 20 May and effectively cut the Allied armies in two. These German advances late on 13 May had hastened a disorganized French retreat which, twenty-four hours later, had been reduced to a rout, opening up a dangerous gap that ultimately the French failed to fill. General Georges Blanchard, commanding

General Maxime Weygand was 73-years-old when he took command of the Allied armies on 17 May

the French First Army, had little choice but to order a retirement to avoid being outflanked, which, in its turn, involved the British I Corps swinging their line back from the Dyle for some six miles to the River Lasane in order to conform to the French retirement. Gamelin was replaced by the 73-year-old General Maxime Weygand on 17 May, but by then the military disaster of 1940 was almost complete and France capitulated on 22 June 1940.

Despite the fact that the BEF was intact and still full of fighting spirit, their movements were now dictated by a wider strategic picture, which had reduced Gamelin's Plan D to ashes and begun to seriously threaten the whole Allied campaign. On 16 May Gort issued his orders for a general withdrawal to the line

The German Army Group A traversed the Ardennes to cross the Meuse at Sedan. Seen here is a Panzer II with a Panzer I about to descend the slope behind.

of the River Senne, orders which were soon replaced with a further retreat to the line of the Escaut, where the BEF paused, until orders sent them back again, this time towards the channel ports, where they were to be evacuated. The BEF's actions along the line of the Escaut are covered fully in the Battleground Europe volume entitled *Battle for the Escaut 1940*.

Chapter 2

A Desperate Situation

Pressure on Cassel and Hazebrouck had begun to develop as early as 17 May, when Gort realized that the BEF positions along the Escaut were in great danger of not only being compromised in the north by the collapse of the Belgians, but also in the south by the panzer divisions of Army Group A. His great fear was the Germans would now drive forward behind his right flank and, with the BEF now fighting on two fronts, his answer took the form of a number of *ad hoc* battle groups, tasked with specific duties of defence. Three of these have a direct bearing on Cassel and Hazebrouck.

Macforce

Under the command of Gort's Director of Intelligence, Major General Noel Mason-MacFarlane, Macforce was created on 17 May. 'Mason-Mac', as he was known throughout the army, was an extraordinary character and was amongst the twenty-one individuals who had been awarded the Military Cross and two bars during the previous conflict. His force consisted of 127 (Manchester) Brigade, commanded by Brigadier John 'Jackie' Smyth, 5/Regiment Royal Horse Artillery (RHA), a battery of guns from 140/ Field Regiment and a battery of anti-tank guns. Mason-Mac also had the armoured cars of the Hopkinson Mission attached to his force, which was under the command of Lieutenant Colonel George 'Hoppy' Hopkinson. Little further is known of their part in the withdrawal to Dunkerque, apart from providing escort duties to GHQ, before they were evacuated on 31 May.

Major General Noel Mason-MacFarlane

Initially ordered to hold the line of the River Scarpe, Macforce gradually found itself being pushed back towards Cassel. MacFarlane lost 127 Brigade on 21 May after it was returned to the 42nd Division and, although it was replaced by 139 Brigade, they too were absorbed into Polforce, which was now operating on Macforce's right flank, and under the command of Major General Henry Curtis.

Thus, Macforce arrived at Cassel – screened by Brigadier Norman's 1/Light

25

Armoured Reconnaisance Brigade - on 24 May without its infantry support and formed a close perimeter defence of the hilltop town where, local historian Camille Taccoen, believes MacFarlane established his HQ in the Casino. Two companies of the 6/York and Lancs held the southern sector, while 100/Field Company and 223/Field Park Company held the northern sector. Five French 75 mm guns were already in the town and these guns were supplemented by one troop from 5/RHA. On 25 May, after the arrival of Brigadier Somerset, Macforce was disbanded and MacFarlane was evacuated to England.

The Hitler Halt Order

Gort's position was now bordering on the desperate. Despite moving elements of the 2nd and 48th Divisions to the La Bassée Canal area, German armoured units secured the crossing of the Aa Canal between St Omer and Aire and were now directly threatening Hazebrouck and Cassel; very little, it seemed, could prevent a total disaster. Amongst those who realized that the BEF was in acute danger was Lieutenant General Alan Brooke, who wrote in his diary on 23 May that, 'nothing short of a miracle can save the BEF now and the end cannot be very far off'.

The miracle – if one can call it that – came about at 12.45pm on 24 May when von Rundstedt ordered *Generaloberst* Günther von Kluge's Fourth Army to halt, an order which was confirmed by Hitler later that day. The directive was simple:

> *On orders of the Fuhrer, the attack to the east of Arras is to be continued with VIII Corps and, to the northwest, II Corps in co-operation with the left wing of Army Group B. The general line Lens-Bethune-Aire-St. Omer-Gravelines will not be crossed northwest of Arras.*

General der Panzertruppen Heinz Guderian, who argued that the order was one of the crucial errors that ultimately lost the war, was, understandably, furious:

> *We were utterly speechless. But since we were not informed of the reasons for this order, it was difficult to argue against it. The Panzer divisions were therefore instructed: hold the line of the canal. Make use of the period for rest and recuperation* [we were told].

Beyond Guderian's fury was the more realistic strategic view held by the German High Command that the Panzers were clearly in need of rest and repair, added to which, it seemed likely that a major French counter-offensive

General der Panzertruppen Heinz Wilhelm Guderian

from the south might extend the already over-stretched Panzer divisions. Also on von Rundstedt's mind was the assault on Boulogne and Calais, by the 2nd and 10th Panzer Divisions, which was proving to be rather costly in terms of men and material. But perhaps more to the point was von Rundstedt's view that Army Group A would be needed for the eventual swing south of the Somme to force the capitulation of the trapped French Army; and that the remnants of the BEF could in fact be finished off by *Generaloberst* Fedor von Bock's Army Group B and the *Luftwaffe*.

What became known as the Hitler halt order effectively enabled Gort to manoeuvre and strengthen his forces and create the Dunkerque Corridor through which the BEF would reach the evacuation beaches at Dunkerque. The halt order was rescinded at

Although von Rundstedt was the architect of the halt order, it was ratified by Adolf Hitler, who only lifted it on 26 May

3.30pm on 26 May, but by then 145 Brigade, or Somerforce as it was labelled by GHQ, had arrived at Cassel and Hazebrouck on BEF's western flank and placed both towns in a state of defence.

Somerforce

The 30-year-old Reverend David Wild was a relative new-boy to 145 Infantry Brigade, in that his life as a master at Eton had been interrupted in 1939 when he became one of the first two Eton masters to be called up. Wild soon found himself administering to the spiritual needs of the territorial officers and men of the 4/Ox and Bucks, a task he undertook with his characteristic thoroughness and sensitivity. On 24 May the brigade was retiring from the Franco-Belgian border, having previously held a section of the River Escaut at Bléharies. Apart from battle casualties, they were already severely under-strength, having lost over 230 men from the 2/Gloucesters and 4/Ox and Bucks when the brigade convoy had been targeted by the *Luftwaffe* near Tournai.

At the time Lieutenant Michael Duncan of the 4/Ox and Bucks felt that the true nature of the disintegration of the Allied Forces in Belgium and France had not really made much of an impact on his men; and although the 48th (South Midland) Division was expecting to take part in a joint operation with the French to attack the flanks of the German breakthrough, the seriousness of the strategic situation facing the BEF was yet to become clear.

It was early on Friday 24 May that orders were received to be ready to move

Brigadier Hon Nigel Fitzroy Somerset

forthwith to Calais. Captain Hugh Saunders, commanding D Company of 1/Bucks, was delighted by this news, declaring that a 'restful task such as the strengthening of the garrison of Calais' would be most welcome after 'the buffeting of the last ten days'. Little was known at the time of the battle that was about to unfold around Calais and the repercussions that were to reverberate through the BEF. David Wild recalled he was with Brigadier Hon Nigel Somerset at Nomain when fresh orders arrived from the 48th Division:

[An officer] *from the 48th Division arrived with fresh orders that the brigade was to go to Hazebrouck* [sic] *and Cassel. Information about enemy movements was obviously very scanty. As far as I remember, what he said roughly was this: Troop carrying transport will arrive this evening. You are to go to Cassel. We don't really know where the enemy are, but we hope you will get there first.*

Captain Eric Jones, the adjutant of the 2/Gloucesters, records that the brigade left Nomain at approximately 9.45pm; and it was while the brigade column was underway for Cassel that a radio message was transmitted to Nigel Somerset from the 46th Division to the effect that he was also to provide a garrison for Hazebrouck. It is worth noting that at the time 145 Brigade were on the road heading for Cassel they were temporarily under the command of Major General Curtis and Polforce. In response, Somerset had little choice but to establish a traffic control post on the D933 leading out of Bailleul and direct the vehicles containing the 1/Bucks along the D944 to Hazebrouck. As the Buckinghamshires were at the rear of the column, it was fate that decreed their move to Hazebrouck, rather than any tactical notion that they were best suited to defend the town.

The trucks carrying Michael Duncan and the men of A Company, 4/Ox and Bucks, to Cassel had lost their way five times during the night, an experience which Duncan found somewhat unnerving, as he 'had no idea where the enemy were and any deviation from the route might well land us amongst them'. Duncan was typical of many of the territorials that made up the bulk of the 4/Ox and Bucks officer's mess; he had joined up in 1934 for no better reason than he liked horses and most of his friends were already part-time soldiers. 'There was' he wrote, 'the rather pleasant sensation of feeling that in some obscure way we were being heroes without having to do anything particularly unpleasant or dangerous to earn the title'. They were words which he admitted later he wished he had never uttered.

Duncan's opinion of the journey to Cassel was undoubtedly shared by Major

Maurice Gilmore, commanding the 2/Gloucesters, who observed, with his usual clipped tone, that 'the battalion reached Cassel after a journey of some vicissitude in the early morning of Saturday, 25 May'. Captain Eric Jones recalled the journey was 'filled with unauthorized halts' but noted he and Gilmore arrived at just after 5.30am. By this time in the campaign the Royal Army Service Corps (RASC) drivers were suffering from almost complete exhaustion, a state that was not improved when it was discovered the majority of the Cassel defence force were missing, presumably after becoming separated in the darkness. In fact it took nearly another hour before the bulk of the two infantry battalions were assembled.

At 7.00am Gilmore and Eric Jones drove up the steep hill towards Cassel and met Lieutenant Colonel Geoffrey Kennedy, commanding the 4/Ox and Bucks, near the communal cemetery by the sharp bend in the road. Here the 'two COs discussed the situation, and, as Brigade HQ had not yet arrived, and in the absence of any orders regarding their deployment, decided, by mutual agreement, to divide Cassel for defence'. This gentleman's agreement appears to have been overturned to some extent by the arrival at 10.45am of Brigadier Somerset, who divided Cassel using the 30 degree gridline, deploying the Gloucesters to the west and the 4/Ox and Bucks to the east. At the same time, he ordered Gilmore to garrison a 'Keep', which included the Gloucester's Battalion HQ in the Place du Général Vandamme.

Apart from the two infantry battalions, Brigadier Somerset was very much aware he was now commanding a mixed force consisting of two troops from 5/Royal Horse Artillery (RHA), the 367/Battery guns from 140/Field Regiment, one and a half batteries from 53/ (Worcestershire Yeomanry) Anti-Tank Regiment, two companies of machine gunners from the 4/Cheshires and a smattering of Royal Engineers from 100/Field Company and 226/Field Company. 223/Field Park Company had already arrived with Macforce. In addition to the troop of gunners from 151/Light Anti-Aircraft Battery, 143/Field Ambulance based itself in one of the buildings in the Grand Place.

145 Brigade Headquarters

On arrival at Cassel, Brigadier Somerset and his staff occupied a small cottage on Chemin de la Cornette near the communal cemetery and established the brigade mess in the cottage next door. At 2.00pm on 27 May the cottage was hit by shellfire and Somerset moved his HQ to another cottage 400 yards away. According to the 145 Brigade war diary, the enemy penetrated the outer defences of Cassel near Dead Horse Corner at about 9.00pm that evening and, although driven back by the 4/Ox and Bucks carriers, they were within a hundred yards of Brigade HQ. Fortunately they were unaware of the close proximity of the building. That evening Somerset moved again; Captain 'Bertie' Lovett, the Gloucesters' Liaison Officer, recalled that they moved to the Gendarmerie on

The Casino at Cassel, standing opposite the Monument des Trois Batailles. It is thought Somerset and 145 Brigade HQ may have resided here briefly.

Rue de Bergues, where Lieutenant Colonel Kennedy had established the 4/Ox and Bucks HQ. 'We proceeded there on foot and I led the way as I had already been up several times by a track which led due north, then cut in towards the Gendamerie.' Lovett says in his account that Brigade HQ moved again that same evening to the Keep, and although the brigade war diary suggests this move was not undertaken until the next day, it does tell us tells us that the staff 'dined most excellently' and celebrated their arrival with a bottle of champagne. What is a little confusing is Captain Eric Jones' map of Cassel, which shows Brigade HQ located at the Casino; there is no direct evidence to suggest Somerset and his staff occupied the building for any length of time.

There is an interesting diary note made by Lieutenant Colonel Douglas Thompson, commanding the East Riding Yeomanry, to the effect that Brigadier Norman (1/ Armoured Light Reconnaissance Brigade) changed the location of his HQ on four occasions and 'Brigadier Somerset changed his even more often'. Thompson maintains that on one occasion Somerset and his HQ were in the cellars of the Hotel de Ville, 'the smell was awful, there was little ventilation and no light but candles. There the staff and signal personnel did their work and issued their orders.' This may well be correct but there is no mention of this location in the brigade war diary and Eric Jones wrote on 29 May that the building had been on fire for two days.

2/Gloucesters

Captain Eric Jones was appointed adjutant on 19 May after Captain Anthony Wilkinson was wounded by machine gun fire near Tournai. It is Jones' detailed

30

account, along with Captain Bill Wilson's description of the B Company dispositions, which give us such a detailed breakdown of the location of the 2/Gloucester platoons. Battalion HQ was initially worked from the 'office truck' until a suitable building was found with an adequate cellar. Temporary accommodation was provided by the large house at the junction of Avenue Albert Mahieu and Route d'Oxeläere near the communal cemetery. At 5.30pm, Major Gilmore moved his Battalion HQ and the Regimental Aid Post (RAP) to the buildings in and around the Banque du Nord – the Keep - on the southern edge of Place du Général Vandamme, where it remained until the withdrawal.

Captain Anthony Wilkinson was evacuated on 19 May

The early deployment of the four companies was altered at 12.30pm on 25 May when Gilmore issued verbal orders to the company commanders as follows: B Company (Captain Bill Wilson) to face north and west along Rue de Watten, to join with C Company of the 4/Ox and Bucks, which was north of the keep. Second Lieutenant George Weightman and 10 Platoon occupied the farm buildings just north and below the main company positions. Wilson's HQ was in a private house on the north side of Rue de Watten.

D Company (Captain Anthony Cholmondeley), with the addition of the Mortar

A map drawn by Captain Eric Jones of the Gloucesters deployment at Cassel

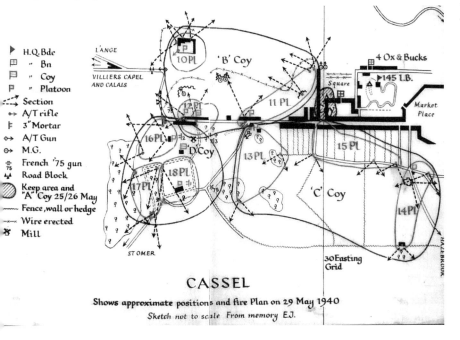

CASSEL

Shows approximate positions and fire Plan on 29 May 1940

Sketch not to scale From memory E.J.

D Company, 2/ Gloucesters occupied the grounds of the Villa de Moulins

Platoon, faced west and south, and occupied the wooded area that was sandwiched between the D11 and the D933. They were directly south of B Company, with their HQ in one of the two the pigeon houses in the grounds of the Villa de Moulins. On the left of D Company, C Company (Captain Esmond Lynn-Allen) faced south, occupying the ground south of Rue Constant Moeneclaery and linking up with A Company of the 4/Ox and Bucks. The fields of fire allocated to Lynn-Allen's three platoons were reduced to some extent by the walled gardens bordering the Rue des Ramparts.

Major Bill Percy-Hardman's A Company was kept in reserve in the Keep, along with the Carrier Platoon. It was only later on Sunday 26 May that A Company, less 8 Platoon, which had been dispatched to the blockhouse west of Le Peckel on the D916, was ordered to proceed to Zuytpeene.

4/Ox and Bucks Light Infantry

Lieutenant Colonel Kennedy established Battalion HQ in the large red brick Gendamerie on the Rue de Bergues, where he and his adjutant, Captain Valentine Fleming, based themselves with HQ Company. On 25 May Kennedy placed B Company (Lieutenant Eric Keen) in reserve and deployed D Company (Captain Charles Clutsom) to cover the Steenvoorde road from Mont de Récollets, while A Company (Captain Lord Patrick Rathcreedan), together with C Company (Major James Graham), took up position along the eastern perimeter. D Company were later dispatched late on 26 May by Lieutenant Colonel Kennedy to Bavinchove, which prompted a further reorganization of the Ox and Bucks defences, involving yet more digging. On their return from Bavinchove, D Company took up a position in between A and C Companies.

Michael Duncan remembers that A Company had been 'allotted a sector of nearly half a mile', with the Company HQ 'in a bomb shattered farm' and recalls standing with Captain Pat Rathcreedan on 27 May watching a German armoured column encircle Bavinchove. Duncan's grandstand view places A Company along the south-eastern perimeter of Cassel, linking up with C Company of the 2/Gloucesters. D Company, on its return from Bavinchove, appears to have been used to plug gaps in the perimeter as and when necessary. In his account of the battle, Second Lieutenant David Wallis, an officer with 145 Brigade Anti-Tank Company, confirms B Company was kept in reserve and A and C Companies were 'halfway down the hill', with A Company astride, what he calls, the Lille road. The C Company HQ was in a row of houses that looked down onto the Grand Place and, from the back, straight over the plain to Dunkerque. The description by David Wild places the building on the Rue Notre Dame, close to the 'ancient archway on the Dunkerque road'.

145 Brigade Anti-Tank Company

At Cassel the brigade anti-tank company was commanded by Captain Edward 'Roger' Dixie, an officer from the 1/Bucks, and was organised into three platoons, each drawing their personnel from the infantry battalions of 145 Brigade. The 1/Bucks Platoon we will deal with in Chapter 5. The Gloucesters' platoon was commanded by Second Lieutenant J Robertson and the 4/Ox and Bucks platoon was under the command of Second Lieutenant

Captain Edward 'Roger' Dixie

David Wallis. The two platoons arrived on the outskirts of Cassel at 4.00am with eight or nine 25mm Hotchkiss anti-tank guns; each gun was allocated to a specific infantry company and the guns were positioned to cover the road blocks on the three major roads that converged on the town.

1/Light Armoured Reconnaissance Brigade

Commanded by Brigadier Charles Norman, the brigade was attached to Macforce on 24 May and consisted of the 1/East Riding Yeomanry and the 1/Fife and Forfar Yeomanry; the third regiment, the 13/18th Royal Hussars, never in fact joined Norman, who was left to operate with the two territorial yeomanry regiments. The East Riding Yeomanry had been in France since February 1940 and moved into

Second Lieutenant David Wallis, taken in 1944 after he had joined the Parachute Regiment

33

The Vickers-Armstrong Mark VIb Light Tank

Belgium on 14 May with the 1/Fife and Forfar Yeomanry. Both regiments were equipped with Mark VIb light tanks and carriers, and were in almost continuous action with German armoured and motorised units prior to their arrival at Cassel.

Having covered the withdrawal of the 44th Division from the Escaut, the East Riding Yeomanry, under the command of Lieutenant Colonel Douglas Thompson, moved to the area of St Sylvestre Cappel and Terdeghem via Hazebrouck. Up until 24 May, each of the four squadrons, A Squadron (Major Horace Wright), B Squadron (Major George Wade), C Squadron (Major Geoffrey Radcliffe) and HQ Squadron (Captain C Smith), had largely operated independently and found themselves acting under orders from several command groups. On 26 May Brigadier Norman ordered them back to Cassel to defend the Mont des Récollets and patrol along the St Omer-Hazebrouck railway line. Regimental HQ was originally established at the Château Masson and Thompson notes in his diary that all that remained of the original twenty-eight tanks and forty-four carriers were nine tanks and eighteen carriers.

The 1/Fife and Forfar Yeomanry was commanded by Lieutenant Colonel Ronald 'Ponto' Sharp. Apart from patrols, the regiment's principle task up until their move north on 28 May was the defence of Mont des Récollets along with the 1/Welsh Guards, the East Riding Yeomanry and 5/RHA. The move north by

The Château Masson, often described as the 'White House', was the temporary headquarters of both 5/RHA and 140/Field Regiment

The Château Masson today

Norman's scratch force not only deprived Mont des Récollets of its garrison, but left the East Riding Yeomanry without its B Echelon transport and 5 Troop (B Squadron, which, at the time, was commanded by Troop Sergeant Major (TSM) Bourne. Thus, three – much depleted – East Riding squadrons were ordered 'to take up positions on the ascent into Cassel', while A Squadron remained defending the road between the Mont des Récollets and Cassel. It is likely that Thompson moved Regimental HQ to the Gendarmerie on Rue de Bergues at this time.

5/Royal Horse Artillery

5/Regiment RHA was formed in November 1938 and consisted of two batteries (K and G), each of twelve 18-Pounder guns, with each battery consisting of three troops. Attached to Macforce on 17 May, the first thing Lieutenant Colonel Alan Durand knew of the move to Cassel was at 8.30am on 24 May, when he was ordered to Macforce HQ at le Motte-au–Bois and given orders to proceed to Cassel via Strazeele. Durand also had command of 367/Battery of 140/Field Regiment; whether this was because the 367/Battery gunners were territorials is unclear, but after arriving at Cassel both units appeared to operate independently. At 1.00pm on 24 May the column was stopped at La Croix Rouge junction – to the west of Cassel - by Lieutenant Colonel Gerald Templar. Templar was the senior staff officer (GSO1) with Macforce and had been directed to divert one battery to Hondeghem. In consultation with Major Robert Rawdon Hoare, the K Battery commander, Durand selected the four guns of Captain Brian Teacher's F Troop, along with eighty men from 5/Battery, 2/Searchlight Regiment, leaving G Battery to establish themselves in the town and on the Mont de Récollets, where D Troop took the western side of the hill and B Troop the east.

Regimental HQ was initially established at Le Coucu but was later moved to the Château Masson, described as the 'white house' and situated between Mont des Récollets and Cassel on the D916. At 10.30am on 27 May, Lieutenant General Pownall arrived at the château to assess the suitability of the building as a possible location for GHQ! Hostile shelling and an assault by enemy tanks evidently

Lieutenant Colonel Gerald Templar, taken after his promotion to lieutenant general in 1946

assisted Pownall in deciding against the move. The war diary recorded rather gleefully that two boxes of stationary and a supply of coloured pencils were left behind. However, with the battle approaching its climax, Regimental HQ followed suit later on 27 May and moved to, what is described in the war diary as, 'a farm', presumably closer to Cassel. The war diary notes that D Troop came into action early on 27 May, firing on German armoured vehicles at Hondeghem, but later came under air attack and reported the loss of two guns. B Troop lost one gun when an ammunition dump was hit by shellfire, killing three men and injuring several others. At 7.00pm on 27 May the remains of K Troop returned from Hondeghem and the next day the regiment left Cassel as part of Brigadier Norman's force.

53/(Worcester Yeomanry)Anti-Tank Regiment, Royal Artillery

The regiment arrived in France with four batteries, each consisting of three troops of four 2-pounder guns under the command of 33-year-old Major Ronald Cartland, the Member of Parliament for King's Norton in Birmingham. 'Ronnie' Cartland was the elder brother of the novelist, Barbara Cartland; his younger brother, Captain James Cartland, was killed serving with the 2/Lincolnshires on 29 May 1940. Second Lieutenant D Woodward commanded A Troop, Troop Sergeant Major (TSM) Prosser led B Troop and Second Lieutenant Bob Hutton-Squire commanded C Troop. The eleven guns of A, B and C Troops were initially

A 2-pounder anti-tank gun and crew pictured during training

dug in around the town, with one gun forming part of a flying squad to deal with any incursions by tanks into the town. Initially six guns from 223/Battery, 53/Anti-Tank Regiment, were sent to Cassel; but on 26 May at least four were sent to Hazebrouck.

On 28 May one troop from 211/Battery, under Major Henry Mercer, arrived at Cassel to reinforce 209/Battery. According to Paul Mace in *Forrard – The Story of the East Riding Yeomanry*, on 29 May Mercer positioned two of his guns at the crossroads at Le Temple and two more on the outskirts of Winnezeele. Clearly the intention was to keep the road open in the event of a withdrawal later that day.

140/Field Regiment, Royal Artillery

In 1940 an artillery regiment of 18/25-pounders had two batteries of twelve guns dispersed amongst three troops, which, in the case of 367/Battery, were lettered D, E and F. On 23 May 367/Battery was detached from 140/Field Regiment – a territorial unit - and became part of Macforce. Present at Cassel were the commanding officer, Lieutenant Colonel Cedris Odling, the battery commander, 47-year-old Major Edward Milton, and Major 'Chris' Christopherson, the second in command.

Regimental HQ was initially at the Château Masson before it was relocated to the vicinity of the Dunkerque Gate, as shown on the map drawn by Eric Jones. Lieutenant Ronald Baxter, serving with F Troop, describes his initial Troop HQ being a cottage below the communal cemetery, which he reached from a track leading off the D916:

> *Immediately opposite the château entrance* [Château Masson] *a narrow lane branched off from the road at right angles, taking another right angled turn a few yards down to the right, then running parallel to the main road*

An 18-pounder gun tractor and limber

A battery of Mark 1 Bofors guns of the type issued to 151/Anti Aircraft Regiment

for 100 yards through a grove of trees and bushes in the direction of the town ... The lane ran clear of the trees, bending to the left, finally ending before a small cottage. We are now, with the cottage facing us, at the foot of the winding road leading to Cassel.

Baxter sited his guns along the track, with D Troop further back and E Troop on his right flank. He also mentions that an anti-aircraft gun was positioned in the field behind him, presumably one of the Bofors guns from 151/Anti-Aircraft Battery. After the fighting on 27 May, Baxter writes that they withdrew F Troop HQ into the town and established a new base 'in a corner estaminet'. This venue may possibly have been in one of the cafés near the Dunkerque Gate. Lieutenant Colonel Odling was wounded on 27 May – with a broken leg from shellfire – and Major Christopherson took over command of the battery. We know from Eric Jones' diary that one section of guns took up positions on 29 May in the Place du Général Vandamme, outside the 2/Gloucesters HQ, and another was in position at the fork in the road near Captain Wilson's B Company HQ.

There are also several reports of French 75mm guns being present at Cassel, having arrived on 24 May and, according to Bombardier Harry Munn from 53/Anti-Tank Regiment, at least one gun was apparently operated by French officers and accounted for several enemy tanks. Another account by Captain Bertie Lovett does confirm the presence of the French guns, but remarks on their ability to contribute to the town's defence! 'I was sent out to verify the truth in

39

The Dunkerque Gate

this – it was true but, unfortunately, not only had the men disappeared but they had taken the firing pins with them rendering the guns useless.'

4/Cheshires

The Cheshires were a divisional machine gun battalion armed with the Vickers, water cooled machine gun, and attached to I Corps as corps troops. Commanded by Lieutenant Colonel John Danson, the battalion was ordered to Cassel on 24 May, where, under the command of 41-year-old Major Edmund Gore-Hickman, it left a composite company of three platoons made up from officers and men from A and C Companies. Several other accounts refer to a quantity of Vickers machine guns that were found abandoned at Cassel and put to good use in bolstering the defences. Apart from the brief account made by Private M Reynolds, the war diary gives little away concerning the location of Company HQ or exactly where the individual platoons were positioned. From Reynolds' account we at least know that there were three platoons, but no specific locality is mentioned. 'We found gun positions and started to dig in. The two sections of 4 Platoon were covering the main roads. No 6 Platoon were on our right and No 12 Platoon on the right of them.'

Captain Bill Wilson, commanding the 2/Gloucester's B Company, was allocated two sections of the Cheshires, whom he positioned just north of 10

40

Men of the 7/Cheshires parade with their Vickers machine guns. The 4/ Cheshires would have been equipped with the same weapons at Cassel

Platoon's farm on the steep ground below Rue de Watten. On 29 May, while 10 Platoon was under heavy shellfire, Wilson writes that the Cheshires abandoned their positions, leaving their machine guns behind them. These men may well have been the group described by Private Reynolds who 'had to leave their position because of shellfire'. It was while Reynolds was at the Advanced Dressing Station (ADS) that he saw Major Gore-Hickman being treated for a serious wound in his back. Captain Eric Jones recalls another section of the

Cheshires was placed in the gap between the Gloucester's B Company and C Company of the 4/Ox and Bucks by Major Gilmore on 29 May.

Royal Engineers

226/Field Company was under the command of Major L J Griffith and arrived at Cassel on 25 May with HQ and No.1 and 3 Sections. No. 2 Section had been detailed to accompany the 1/Bucks to Hazebrouck. 223/Field Park Company, under the command of Captain R A Elliott, was also present at Cassel, having arrived with Macforce. They prepared roadblocks to the north-east of Cassel before proceeding to Wormhout on 28 May. 100/Field Company, under the command of Major George Whitehead, was attached to Macforce on 17 May and were engaged in preparing and fortifying infantry and gunnery posts on the vulnerable north-west slopes of Cassel. On 24 May Sapper Leslie Davies became the Company's first casualty when he was killed during an air attack on Cassel. The company's last task was an unsuccessful attempt to blow a bridge on 27 May on the main Cassel to Dunkerkque road by Lieutenant Mercer and his section. It was here that 36-year-old Driver James Ware was mortally wounded.

143/Field Ambulance

Apart from Eric Jones' map, which shows 143/Field Ambulance based in the Grand Place near Rue d'Aire, the war diary is again frustratingly brief in its description of the Cassel detachment. The unit arrived on 24 May, but was ordered to remain outside the town until the next morning, when Lieutenant Colonel William Marsden established an ADS under the command of Major J G Lawson. There is a fleeting mention of nineteen casualties suffered by the ADS staff at Cassel on 27 May and a short sentence noting that the unit – less the ADS at Cassel - left for Oost Cappel at 9.30am that morning. On 28 May, Mardsen left Cassel for Hondschoote and then proceeded to Dunkerque, where he and the surviving members of the unit were evacuated on 29 May.

1/Welsh Guards

Technically the battalion was not part of either Macforce or Somerforce, as it was under the command of GHQ, and had previously been part of the Arras garrison, from where they withdrew on 24 May. It was during this withdrawal that Lieutenant Hon Christopher Furness was awarded the Victoria Cross. The Guards, under the command of Lieutenant Colonel Felix Copland-Griffiths, arrived at Cassel during the morning of 26 May and took over the defence of a sector of Mont des Récollets . The 1/Fife and Forfar war diary records that the Welsh Guards were 'removed for another task' at 11.00am on 27 May, which turned out to be a very temporary move to Houtkerque, as they had returned to their positions on Mont des Récollets at 10.30pm on the same day. The language amongst the guardsmen must have been colourful! Finally, on 28 May, the battalion placed themselves under Brigadier Norman's command and proceeded north with Norman's scratch force to Socx, where German armoured units were harassing the western flank of the Dunkerque Corridor.

German Armoured Units

The German units ranged against Cassel were formidable. The 6th Panzer Division was commanded by *General der Panzertruppe* Werner Kempf, who organized his division into three *Kampfgruppes* - battle groups. As soon as the Hitler halt order was lifted on the evening of 26 May, both *Kampfgruppe* von Esebeck and *Kampfgruppe* Koll, which was built around *Oberstleutnant* Richard Koll's Panzer Regiment 11, headed directly for Cassel the next morning. It was *Oberst* Hans-Karl von Esebeck who carried out the attack on Cassel on 27 May from the south and east – apparently with little infantry support - and lost heavily to the British anti-tank crews. thereafter he was given to a secondary role in support of Richard Koll's attack. By the time that

Oberstleutnant Richard Koll

Koll approached Cassel he had an armoured strength of twenty Panzer IIs, twenty-five Panzer IVs and seventy Panzer 35(t)s. The third group, *Kampfgruppe* von Ravenstein, was responsible for shelling Cassel on 24 May before the division was withdrawn to the canal. With the lifting of the halt order, *Oberst* Johann von Ravenstein, along with elements of IR 4, Panzer battalion 65 and AR 76, were tasked with by-passing Cassel and Hondeghem to advance on Caëstre; on 29 May, they cut the road from Poperinghe to Proven and made the first contact with Army Group B when they met a motorised patrol from IR17

Oberst Hans-Karl von Esebeck

43

The Panzerkampfwagen 35(t) was a Czechoslovak-designed light tank and saw combat in the early years of the war

The Panzerkampfwagen IV saw extensive service and was the only German tank to remain in continuous production throughout the war

Chapter 3

The Battle for Cassel

Shortly after dawn on 25 May, when the first troops of 145 Brigade began to arrive, it must have been instantly apparent that the town had suffered badly from air raids and German shelling over the previous twenty-four hours. George McNab, a major with 5/Casualty Clearing Station, passed through the town on 23 May and noted the devastation caused by German bombing. 'Not a soul was to be seen: the most prominent feature of the [Grand] Place was a burned out motor bus, and several of the lovely old buildings which had stood around were now lying in heaps in the road.' Two days later David Wild noted the bend in the road by the communal cemetery, where Gilmore and Kennedy had met, 'was not a very cheering sight, as all over the road were the remains of wagons, guns and horses'. It was a spectacle that greeted practically every man of the mixed force of infantry, sappers and gunners as they wound their way up the hill into the centre of the town. When the East Riding Yeomanry passed the cemetery on their way up into the town, they were surprised to see a number of bodies strewn across the road. There was, however, a general feeling of relief when it was discovered the 'sea of blood' which covered the road, was in fact red wine escaping from one of the horse drawn limbers. The next day Wild helped to bury the bodies of the French who were scattered about the road and, with the assistance of the 4/Ox and Bucks pioneers, cleared away the dead horses. Thereafter the bend in the road became known amongst the troops as Dead Horse Corner.

David Wild, pictured at Oflag VII in 1941

The 25 May was relatively quiet, which gave the arriving troops plenty of time to dig in and prepare the town for the inevitable attack by German forces. Four hourly patrols by the 1/Fife and Forfar Yeomanry were established on the Steenvoorde-Cassel road and the Gloucesters' Carrier Platoon, under Sergeant I Kibble, patrolled as far as the railway line. It was the lull before the storm. Like many of his contemporaries, Major Gilmore was largely unaware of the critical nature of the situation facing the BEF:

> Reports had been received earlier of isolated German tanks having broken
> through ahead of the main enemy thrusts further inland, and now at large on

the coast or in the vicinity of Cassel and its neighbourhood, but nothing was known to have occurred which would eventually lead to the evacuation at Dunkirk. The first two days (25 and 26 May) were ones of rest. It is true that this period was mainly occupied with constructing defences and preparing for eventualities, but at least it was possible to have a proper night's rest, comfortable and sufficient meals and the opportunity to reorganize.

Maurice Gilmore had been elevated to battalion command on 15 May, after Nigel Somerset had replaced Brigadier Archie Hughes in command of 145 Brigade; his apparent relaxed attitude was not necessarily one shared by all the 4/Ox and Bucks, who, after a morning of digging on 25 May, were then ordered to leave the positions they had so laboriously prepared and dig completely new ones on the eastern perimeter of Cassel. Their mood was not improved by their midday 'meal'; Lieutenant Michael Duncan recalled the look of disgust on his men's faces when they were served up with a slice of fried meatloaf and a mug of tea! He notes that it was not until dusk on 25 May that the defences were completed and the men were able to 'sink down exhausted into their [weapon] pits'. David Wild was the first to agree that food was getting very short, 'meals consisted entirely of food collected from houses. Bread no longer existed and the

The officers of the 4/Ox and Bucks. Pictured left to right – Captain M Fleming, Lieutenant Duncan is third left and Lieutenant Keen is seventh from the left. Second Lieutenant Ruck Nightingale, Captain Lansdell RAMC and Second Lieutenant Clerke Brown, are the last three on the right.

chief item of diet seemed to be sweet wafer biscuits and a form of confectionary known to the troops as 'rubbers.'

Sunday 26 May

Dawn saw a resumption of patrols out to the west of Cassel in an effort to discover exactly where the German forces were. Second Lieutenant Mortimer Lanyon from 5/RHA was sent out with one 18-pounder to support a reconnaissance patrol of the 1/Fife and Forfar Yeomanry, who had been dispatched to the Forêt de Clairmarais. Lanyon positioned his gun by a farm at le Tom on the D26 where tanks 'of an unknown nationality' had been seen that morning. These tanks may have crossed the canal at Watten and were certainly in advance of the main body of the 6th Panzer Division, who were still technically immobilized by the Hitler halt order.

Meanwhile, back at Cassel, Sergeant Kibble had been ordered to patrol beyond the railway line and report the situation around the wooded area west of l'Hey. Accordingly, at 9.45am, the Carrier Platoon, along with one anti-tank gun and a dispatch rider (DR) left Cassel and headed west. After discovering Zuytpeene was clear of the enemy, the patrol moved on towards l'Hey, where enemy tanks were seen near the village crossroads. Before the anti-tank gun could be brought

The Universal Carrier, also known as the Bren Gun Carrier. Each infantry battalion was equipped with one platoon of carriers

into action it was hit by shellfire from one of the tanks, the gun crew scattering under a hail of hostile machine gun fire. Abandoning the gun, Sergeant Kibble ordered a withdrawal to Zuytpeene and sent two sections back to Cassel to report to Major Gilmore. Gilmore's impatient reply was terse and to the point – they were to counter attack and recover the gun and crew immediately.

Second Lieutenant Lanyon, still at le Tom, recalled Kibble's carriers arrived at his location at 1.00pm:

I was about to shell the copse [at l'Hey] *when two hostile tanks appeared near it. I opened fire and they disappeared into it. I shelled the copse and waited, and later my No.1 reported he could see tanks now coming down a hedge. At the same time a third tank, which we could not see, opened fire on us from a different area. I engaged the two tanks at 2,000 yards approx, and both were put out of action. The third tank escaped in another direction.*

Lanyon's timely intervention allowed the Fife and Forfar Yeomanry to cover Kibble's carriers in recovering the gun and crew. Mortimer Lanyon was delighted to receive confirmation of his two 'kills' and, having covered the withdrawal, returned to Cassel at 7.00pm.

Not satisfied with his current arrangements, Brigadier Nigel Somerset looked for an opportunity to break the momentum of the German advance. Consequently, he fixed his attentions on the villages of Zuytpeene and Bavinchove to the west of Cassel and a blockhouse on the northerly Dunkerque road at Le Peckel. At 2.30pm, while Sergeant Kibble was engaged in recovering the anti-tank gun at l'Hey, Second Lieutenant Roy Cresswell, commanding A Company's 8 Platoon, was sent out to reconnoitre the suitability of the blockhouse as a defensive position. His subsequent report highlighted the limitations of the incomplete blockhouse and the amount of work that would be necessary to ensure its use as a strongpoint. Nevertheless, Cresswell was dispatched at 9.30pm, with his platoon, to occupy the blockhouse and hold it 'at all costs'.

An hour later, the remaining platoons of A Company, under 34-year-old Major Bill Percy-Hardman, were ordered to occupy Zuytpeene and Lieutenant Colonel Kennedy of the Ox and Bucks was ordered to find a company to occupy Bavinchove. As D Company moved out to Bavinchove their place was taken up by B Squadron East Riding Yeomanry, who, like the infantry, were digging new positions until well after dark.

The Blockhouse at le Peckel

Second Lieutenant Roy Cresswell and 8 Platoon arrived at the blockhouse during the late evening of 26 May. Early the next morning the platoon worked hard to block up the entrances and remove the builder's hut and scaffolding before the enemy attack that Cresswell was expecting later that day:

> At 6.00pm the Germans were seen advancing in open order across the western skyline. The side entrance was immediately shut and a heavy fire brought to bear on the advancing enemy, upon which several casualties must have been inflicted at a range of 600 yards. Between 7.00pm and 8.00pm a furious attack was launched against us, which was beaten off, the only lasting effect being that one nearby haystack was fired by tracer. This proved to be advantageous to us, since it burnt all night, and the light this caused made the work of the look-outs slightly easier. In the attack the Germans used a type of shell which was about 2-inches long and which burst inside the blockhouse. Part of one of these hit L/Cpl Ruddy, [Dennis Ruddy] who was severely wounded in the head and throat.

Tuesday May 28 was relatively quiet for Cresswell and his men, no enemy attacks took place, although mechanized columns were seen moving east of Cassel, leading to much speculation as to what was happening to the battalion on the hill.

The blockhouse at le Peckel

Everything changed the next morning, a day which Cresswell described as 'one of the worst days we had experienced in the blockhouse'. It began at about 9.00am with the appearance of Captain Derick Lorraine, a wounded British artillery officer, who was seen hobbling on a crutch shouting 'wounded British officer here'. Already a PoW, Lorraine had been turned out of an ambulance by his captors. Forced to approach the blockhouse at gunpoint, Lorraine made every effort to indicate there were Germans on the roof attempting to start a fire with petrol in the well of the unfinished turret housing. Cresswell remembered that he responded immediately and that Lorraine replied 'do not reply' in a lower voice:

> When he reached the east side he looked down at a dead German and said out loud, 'There are many English and Germans like that round here.' At the same time he looked up at the roof of the blockhouse, an action which seemed to indicate German presence on the roof. With that he hobbled out of sight.

Second Lieutenant Roy Cresswell was awarded the MC for his stand at le Peckel

Lorraine's silent gesturing was not lost on Creswell. As smoke filled the blockhouse the defending Gloucesters donned gas masks while they struggled to put out the fire, Cresswell remarking that they [the Germans] had failed again to drive them out but in the process had improved the warmth inside the blockhouse! Their battle came to an end on 30 May, heavy weapons were brought up and their continued resistance seemed

49

An aerial photograph of the modern day Zuypteene with Cassel in the background.

futile, particularly as nothing had been heard from Cassel. They had held the blockhouse for three days, keeping the smoke from the fire at bay by the use of an old quilt damped with water from the blockhouse well and demonstrated a grit and determination worthy of their famous cap badge. As Cresswell and his platoon were being marched away as prisoners, the fire continued to burn for the next week as a constant reminder of a tenacious defence.

Zuytpeene

At 8.00pm on 26 May, Majors Gilmore and Percy-Hardman left Cassel to reconnoitre Zuytpeene; but it was not until 2.45am the next morning that A Company, with its two remaining platoons and an anti-tank gun from 145 Brigade Anti-Tank Company, left Cassel. Private Alfred 'Sam' Tickner was Major Percy-Hardman's driver and, according to his account, Company HQ was established in a house with a deep cellar just inside the village where there was room to park the company vehicles. Percy-Hardman came from a family already ravaged by the casualties of war, losing his father to shellfire in 1917 when he was still a boy. There would be further anguish in March 1945 when his younger brother, Cecil, was destined to die of wounds in Holland.

Zuytpeene in 1940 was not much smaller than it is today but, even so, the two platoons were stretched to cover the whole perimeter. Private H Vaughan was serving in 9 Platoon, under 25-year-old Platoon Sergeant Major (PSM) Boswell Oxtoby, which was positioned in and around the village near Company HQ, while Sergeant Nix, who was commanding 7 Platoon, was holding the railway line. Oxtoby's Platoon HQ was at the church and it was probably his men that were experiencing problems with preparing the village for defensive action.

Captain Eric Jones writes in his diary that A Company had great difficulty in convincing the local population that the arrival of the Germans was imminent and they should vacate their houses forthwith. However, the arrival of a German motorcyclist at the village crossroads, with an officer in the sidecar, would have finally convinced even the most doubtful that fighting was about to begin. Corporal Leach and Private Stevens opened fire immediately, killing the motorcyclist. Vaughan described the opening shots of the battle:

> *The officer dashed to cover and got away. We then heard tanks entering the village and they started shelling the house we were in and scored a direct hit. Rifle fire was also directed onto the house and Corporal Holner was wounded. We remained in the house. The rifle pits we had made were occupied by some French soldiers who were retiring in front of the Germans and firing back at them. The Germans continued shelling these trenches and the house.*

Vaughan writes that after PSM Oxtoby was wounded, he and Private Price were instructed to get back to Cassel and ask for reinforcements; a cross country journey that involved running the gauntlet through the encircling German units. When he left the village Vaughan is quite sure there were only about four unwounded men left in his platoon and there was no sign of Major Percy-Hardman or CSM Brown. Passing Company HQ the two men saw it had been 'completely demolished' by shellfire. They reached Cassel by nightfall and were told not to return to the company.

At roughly the same time, Privates 'Sam' Tickner and 'Jugs' Bennett from Company HQ volunteered to return to Cassel to report on the deteriorating situation at Zuytpeene. Whether they left Company HQ before Vaughan and Price were clear of the village is not known, but both sets of men did reach the comparative safety of the British lines at Cassel at about 7.00pm. Reporting to Major Gilmore in 'an exhausted state', Tickner and Bennett – who were certain Major Percy-Hardman was dead – told Gilmore the company had taken heavy casualties and was completely surrounded.

In many respects the demise of A Company was a foregone conclusion and one that must have occurred to both Gilmore and Percy-Hardman during their reconnaissance the previous day. Gilmore's repeated attempts to send orders to Percy-Hardman to withdraw failed to penetrate the German encirclement of the village, and his final instruction to Second Lieutenant Thomas Reeve Tucker to contact any survivors from A Company was almost an act of desperation. Gilmore ordered a similar unsuccessful attempt to reach the le Peckel blockhouse late on 27 May. Reeve-Tucker left Cassel at 9.30pm only to return five hours later, having failed to reach Zuytpeene. In actual fact Percy-Hardman was still very much alive, although his company had been reduced to a handful of survivors and one Bren gun and forced back to the cellar at Company HQ. With the enemy throwing grenades into the cellar and the building in flames, they finally surrendered at 7.00pm.

Bavinchove

One mile east of Zuytpene, D Company of the 4/Ox and Bucks were also coming under attack at Bavinchove. Commanded by Captain Charles Clutsom, it was not until early on 27 May that they came into contact with the men of I/Pz11. From their vantage point above Rue des Ramparts at Cassel, Michael Duncan and Captain Lord 'Pat' Rathcreedan were able to watch the approach of a German armoured column:

As Pat, the Company Commander, and I stood watching for signs of the enemy we saw, winding out along the road from St Omer to Bavinchove, a long column of enemy tanks preceded by motor cyclists and armoured cars and followed by infantry in half tracks ... suddenly the head of the column broke, as if splintered, with pieces flying in every direction as they came under fire from the defenders of Bavinchove. For a while there was a lull, as if orders were being given and then, methodically, inexorably, the encircling movement began.

As part of the defences, Clutsom ordered two locomotives and their rolling stock to block any movement across the railway line towards Cassel. *Hauptmann* Jurgens described the opening attack:

We progress slowly, feeling the ground ... In the village a railway crosses the road, which is our axis of advance towards Cassel, two locomotives are placed there to stand in our way. I place two Panzer IVs to ensure our safety. Outfielder grenadiers are posted near the houses ... Colonel von Esebeck asks me to attack, I am about to do so when the locomotives have been cleared away. Suddenly, cracks [British rifle and machine gun fire] *around us, everyone seeks shelter, the Panzer IVs open fire. Two English caterpillars* [Carriers] *are destroyed. The commander of the motorised company, Oberstleutnant von Sekendorff, arrives at my position. In front of us we have English who fiercely defend.*

Second Lieutenant David Wallis, does not say if he was present at Bavinchove, but his diary does confirm that D Company were attacked by motorcycle troops, troops in lorries and about six tanks:

The front section of D Company were attacked first on its flanks, the enemy stalking it. Grenades were thrown by both sides. At about 9.30am, when the section withdrew across the line to its rear platoon, it found the enemy were on its right flank and pushing round behind the whole company.

The single 25mm anti-tank gun was in position on the railway line firing across the road and, Wallis writes, four armoured fighting vehicles were put out of action. However, once the Germans began outflanking them on the right, hostile machine gun fire was directed straight down the railway line, killing 21-year-old Private George Blake and wounding two other men. Abandoning the damaged gun, the remaining gun crew withdrew to Cassel. In the meantime, D Company fought on and, after sustaining heavy casualties, fell back on Cassel, with George Clutsom bringing a number of wounded men back in a small Morris Eight under heavy fire.

Monday 27 May

Leaving aside the events taking place around the three outposts of Bavinchove, Zuytpeene and le Peckel, the battle around Cassel began with enemy mortar fire from the south, which increased in intensity as the ranging bursts got nearer to the Cassel perimeter. Earlier that morning David Wild was witness to the unpleasantness of war when he watched the occupants of vehicles carrying C and D Companies of the 9/Sherwood Foresters debussing in the Grand Place. Standing outside the Ox and Bucks C Company HQ, he watched with horror as a Junkers 87b 'Stuka' scored a direct hit on the leading vehicle. Wild rushed down to the shattered vehicles to 'find a terrible shambles' as the casualties were collected and taken to the 143/Field Ambulance building in the square.

At around midday, Ronald Baxter and F Troop of 140/Field Regiment were coming under increasing pressure as German tanks appeared a mere 300 yards from their gun positions and bracketed mortar fire began falling on the D916. Engaging the hostile tanks over open sights, a duel between tank and field gun ensued, during which Lieutenant Jack May was badly wounded in the shoulder and arm, and Sergeant Harry Swindle was killed. Swindle had only just been

German troops approaching Cassel

53

Camarades!

Telle est la situation!

En tout cas, la guerre est finie pour vous!
Vos chefs vont s'enfuir par avion.
A bas les armes!

British Soldiers!

Look at this map: it gives your true situation!
Your troops are entirely surrounded —
stop fighting!
Put down your arms!

The propaganda leaflet dropped on
British troops defending Cassel and
Hazebrouck

treated at the RAP for a wound in his foot by Captain Lacey when he was hit again and died almost immediately. Moments later Lieutenant Charles Bennett was wounded with a shell splinter in his back.

As the German tanks worked their way into the grounds of the Château Masson, it soon became clear that their intention was to force their way onto the low saddle of ground joining Mont des Récollets with Cassel. In what seemed to be an eleventh-hour appearance, Second Lieutenant Charlie Clerke Brown's carriers and a party of the Ox and Bucks, led by CSM Cecil Bailey from A Company, arrived and cleared the Germans out of the château grounds. But the situation remained desperate; Clerke Brown's carriers were continually on the move, engaging German armoured vehicles and machine gunning pockets of enemy infantry, while the 27-year-old Captain Michael Fleming 'who seemed completely unmoved by any form of fire, came riding on his motor-cycle over the rubble looking as if he were out for a Sunday afternoon ride, and distributing cigarettes or other luxuries which he had discovered'. Michael Fleming was the son of Major Valentine Fleming, who was killed in 1917, and the youngest of three boys, one of whom was Ian Fleming, the novelist who wrote the James Bond novels.

It was around this time that the Cassel defenders were treated to what Michael Duncan called 'fresh entertainment in the form of a leaflet raid':

> The leaflets were very amateurish and consisted of a rough plan of the area, showing the town to be surrounded, and underneath the caption, in French and English ...Many were collected as souvenirs but the total effect was summed up by the man who remarked: 'Just as we were running out of [toilet] paper too. How did they guess?

As the battle developed, the anti-tank gun crews found no shortage of targets and, as was the case at Hazebrouck, it is doubtful the garrison could have held out for so long without the fifteen 2-pounders of the Worcestershire Yeomanry and the 18-pounders of 367/Battery. There were, however, limitations. Captain Eric Jones recalled his frustration at being told the 18-pounders were unable to elevate sufficiently to hit targets below the hill, he also remarks that companies 'repeatedly asked for artillery support and even though targets were pinpointed on the map, the gunners were either not available or could not give any support'. Nevertheless, the gunners inflicted heavy losses on enemy armour. Bombardier Harry Munn, a 209/Battery gunner, was in Second Lieutenant Bob Hutton-Squire's C Troop and was amongst the first to spot twenty-four tanks in line abreast coming towards the British lines. Private Frank Barber wondered if they might be British, but the swastika flags draped on the front of each tank soon identified them as hostile. Standing behind the gun, Hutton-Squire called out 'tanks in your area Bombardier'. But Munn had seen them and the crew were already preparing the gun for firing as the enemy vehicles reached a small wood at the base of the ridge. With the first tank heading in their direction, Munn's first shot missed its target and the second bounced off the tank's armour:

Bombardier Harry Munn

By now the tank was less than 100 yards from our position and we still could not penetrate its armour. The only thing I could think of was that the wheels that propelled the tank tracks were unprotected and so I shouted to Frank 'Hit the bastard in the tracks, Frank'. The gun muzzle dipped slightly and just as the tank moved we fired, hitting the track propulsion wheels and the tank halted abruptly, swinging to one side. Still full of fight, they turned their gun in our direction and fired again, hitting the bank in front of the gun. Our next shell must have disabled the turret as they opened the escape hatch and ran for their lives back towards their lines. George Prosser, our Troop Sergeant, had left his Troop HQ when he saw we were about to engage the tanks, and laid down by the gun, taking pot shots with his rifle. He hit the last German to leave the tank, who fell down by the side of his tank. The other two tanks that came through with the one we had just stopped were on the right and left of our position. I decided to engage the one on the left as it was close to the outskirts of the town and firing mortars at a target in our lines. It was a perfect target silhouetted against a small hillock. I gave the necessary commands – direction – range – and a zero lead fire. Frank pressed the firing pedal and this time the shell penetrated the armour, exploded inside the tank and blew it into small pieces as its own ammunition went up. There were no survivors. The third tank had not moved from the point where we had first sighted it and its turret moved slowly round searching for our gun. I re-laid the gun on the new target, gave the order 'Fire!'. Bill Vaux had already loaded and Frank followed the tank traversing left and right as it searched for our position. Frank talked to himself as he followed the target, 'Keep still you bastard' and as the tank paused for a second he fired, completely destroying this one as we had the previous one.

Second Lieutenant Wallis' diary notes that from his position about forty tanks were seen approaching Cassel at 10.30 on 27 May. Some of the tanks were reported to be 'medium light' and others 'medium heavy', suggesting the tanks may have been a mixture of Panzer II and Panzer IVs:

Four tanks were smoking after about fifteen minutes and there were about eight stationary ones deserted by their crews. It appeared that after one shot at a tank, the crew were very apt to get out and run. At this time the fighting became very heavy from other tanks and light machine guns. Captain Dixie was killed, but [the] gun remained unhurt ... By 3.00pm there were eighteen tanks in front without their crews.

The 24-year-old Captain Roger Dixie was a third year veterinary student when he was called up in August 1939 and had taken over the firing of the No.8 Gun when it was hit. He died of wounds thirty minutes later. Earlier, on the A Company (4/Ox and Bucks) front, tanks were seen advancing towards their positions. The anti-tank gun immediately engaged them but was destroyed by a direct hit after

A Panzer 35(t) destroyed by British anti-tank fire at the junction of the Route d'Oxelaëre and the Ste-Marie-Cappel road. The tavern behind the tank was converted into a private house in 1970.

The .55 Boys Anti-Tank Rifle was names after its creator, Captain H C Boys and was only effective against light armour at 100 yards range. The recoil from the weapon could cause neck strains and bruised shoulders to the uninitiated

some two hours. By this time, writes Wallis, 'the tanks had suffered pretty badly and withdrew'.

It still remains unclear as to exactly how many tanks were destroyed on 27 May but some indication was given by Captain QM Randolph Brasington, who maintained at least eight or nine were knocked out in the Gloucesters' area, a number he attributed solely to the work of the Boys anti-tank rifle. If one adds the tanks claimed to have been destroyed by the gunners and the men of the Ox and Bucks, then the total increases to a number in excess of forty.

In the Gloucesters' B Company area, Second Lieutenant Julian Fane, commanding 12 Platoon, was tasked with fortifying the residential houses on Rue de Watten, and felt 'things were very awkward as the civilians had not all cleared out of the town'. He and his men spent some time turning people out of their houses in order to secure them against attack and spent most of the 26 May 'pit-propping, sand bagging, boarding up windows (inside), caging, digging a second exit to our cellar, making holes in the walls for communication and slits for firing'. The 19-year-old Fane was a regular soldier who had only just graduated from Sandhurst and joined the battalion on 14 May after being transferred from the 5/Gloucesters. His platoon occupied the most westerly buildings on the north side of Rue de Watten, from where they had good sight of the farm buildings below them, held by 27-year-old Second Lieutenant George Weightman and 10 Platoon. PSM Ernest Morgan and 11 Platoon were a little further east along the street, close to the fork with the D933. Shelling began late in the morning of 27 May and around midday, a direct hit on Company HQ on Rue de Watten, buried Captain Bill Wilson's belongings in 'about four inches of brick dust'. Fortunately there were no casualties but Wilson slept in the cellar thereafter!

On the south side of Rue de Watten, D Company had established its Company HQ in one of the two *pigeonaires* situated in the extensive grounds of the Villa de Moulins. After a period of intense machine gun and rifle fire which appeared to originate in D Company's area, reports reached Wilson that a tank had penetrated the grounds and some of the D Company forward positions had been abandoned. Running across the road, Wilson was disturbed to find about forty men of D Company 'standing like lost sheep in the lane opposite my HQ', which led down to the D Company area:

Thinking that something must have happened to Cholmondeley, I managed to get all D Company back into the grounds into positions of some sort. I

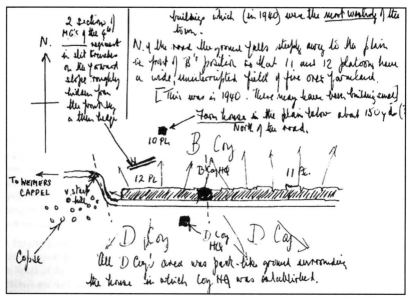

A map drawn by Captain Bill Wilson of the B Company deployment at Cassel. PSM Morgan and 11 Platoon occupied the buildings east of Company HQ as far as the fork in the road while 2/Lt Fane and 12 Platoon was on the left of Company HQ, which in 1940, were the most westerly houses in the town. 2/Lt Weightman and 10 Platoon were to the north.

The farmhouse at George Weightman's farm

found Cholmondeley in his HQ surrounded by wounded ... [he] told me that his anti-tank rifles were ineffectual against the tank in the grounds, but I couldn't get clear information from him as to where exactly the tank was; he was very much upset.

Second Lieutenant Fane takes up the story:

While the mêlée was going on, [Lieutenant] French, the Intelligence Officer (IO), asked me to get an anti-tank rifle and try and engage the tank at close range. I called for a volunteer, who jumped at the job, for they were all very keen. I was acting as his No.2. We crept up to within 50 yards of its position and got ready to fire the rifle. The Mortar Platoon must have been told to deal with the tank as well, for just as we were going to fire, 2 bombs burst just in front of us and blew a hole in the back of the man with me [Private Palmer] and twisted up the anti-tank rifle like a piece of barbed wire.

Fane fails to mention that Wilson and CSM Robinson were also part of his party. Wilson says four other mortar bombs followed in rapid succession and it was only after they had withdrawn and he had climbed to the top of the *pigeonaires* that he saw the tank 'at the end of the grounds, conning tower [sic] open and smoke pouring out of it'. The tank had fallen prey to an anti-tank gun, possibly from 53/Anti-Tank Regiment.

As the attack on D Company continued, it became obvious that the enemy were attempting to establish a post in the south western corner of the grounds. Led by Captain Cholmondeley, a party of six men counter attacked and drove the enemy off without loss to themselves and without reporting the presence of other tanks in the grounds; which casts doubts on the notion that there were two further tanks in the grounds still engaging D Company. Fortunately, by 5.00pm the enemy were seen to be withdrawing and the shelling reduced, although Bill Wilson thought it continued 'well towards dusk'.

Gilmore and Eric Jones toured the Gloucesters' company defences that evening, remarking there were a considerable number of casualties and an 'appreciable number of enemy tanks lying derelict in open country, particularly opposite C Company', which he attributed to good shooting with the Boys anti-tank rifle. That night it rained hard, which put out some of the fires in Cassel but, as Michael Duncan observed, 'it did nothing to improve the conditions of the men crouching in their slit trenches or peering out into the darkness, expecting the attack to be resumed at any minute'. On the Mont des Récollets , Corporal Moore, serving with B Squadron of the East Riding Yeomanry, was soaked through to the skin and the slit trenches they had dug were continually filling up with water. Snatching a few minutes desperately needed sleep, his tin helmet filled with water, which cascaded over him as he placed it back on his head. The full content of his response was not recorded!

59

The meeting at the Hôtel du Sauvage

Apparently unaware of the impeding storm about to break on Cassel, an early morning meeting was arranged on 27 May at the Hôtel du Sauvage between Lieutenant General Sir Robert Adam and General Bertrand Fagalde, with the intention of agreeing the perimeter line for the defence of Dunkerque. Lieutenant Colonel Hon Robert Bridgeman, a staff officer serving with Adam, was one of the first to arrive:

> *I got safely to Cassel, parked the car in a side street and went to the Hôtel du Sauvage in the square. It had been hit by a shell and the staff had evidently bolted the day before, leaving the cloths on the tables in the dining room where the conference was to be held ... General Adam had arrived just before me, fortunately Fagalde also came early, and armed with my precious map, I got them both together on a side table, used by waiters in better times, and they had about ten minutes settling the occupation of the Dunkerque perimeter.*

The meeting – which by its very nature has to be considered one of the most vital that took place in those final days of the campaign - is not mentioned in any other

The Hôtel du Sauvage as it is today

account of the Cassel fighting and must have passed almost unnoticed by the garrison. It appears that Fagalde and General Louis Koeltz, representing General Weygand, were largely unaware of Gort's intention to evacuate the BEF and, as the meeting broke up to the tune of a German artillery bombardment, Fagalde writes that he was left with the distinct feeling that the British were abandoning their allies and leaving them to fend for themselves.

Tuesday 28 May

Enemy mortar and shell fire began quite early, which by 10.00am were falling on Cassel at a rate of one per minute and hardly slackened for the whole day. Eric Jones, in his meticulously kept diary, recorded that at times he counted six or seven shells per minute. Captain Bill Wilson reported a direct hit by a 6-inch shell on one of the company cookhouses, which heralded an attack on 10 Platoon later in the afternoon:

> *Tanks approached our position along the road from the west. At the La Croix fork one appeared from behind the houses. At the time I was at 10*

Destroyed vehicles, probably from 140/Field Regiment, in Rue du Maréchal Foch

An abandoned 18-pounder gun tractor in Place du Général Vandamme

Platoon HQ. The anti-tank rifle was brought into action. Later a few infantry appeared along the hedges about 400 yards away; they were fired upon and withdrew.

A German dispatch rider

Later in the evening a German despatch rider (DR), *Gefreiter* Josef Schmoetzer, was shot in the B Company area and, when examined by the Gloucesters' Intelligence Officer, Lieutenant Gerry French, gave a good deal of information regarding the supposed imminent withdrawal of his regiment of field artillery. His appearance was too good to be true, and the suspicion he was a deliberate 'plant' was confirmed the next morning when the shelling began again at 8.00am and B Company HQ received a direct hit, killing the Signal Corporal and Bill Wilson's Batman.

Wednesday 29 May

Shelling and mortaring began early on all company fronts around Cassel, but the main action of the day was on the Gloucesters' B Company Front. Lance Corporal J Eldridge was at Company HQ when a runner arrived from 10 Platoon:

Between 11.00am and noon a runner from that platoon came to Coy HQ and reported that 2nd Lieutenant Weightman had been killed. And the platoon mortared out of its position. All the platoon were either killed, missing or wounded.

It was not entirely true as, when Captain Bill Wilson and the company stretcher bearers rushed down the hill to the farm, they discovered Corporal Christopher Waite and three men had remained behind and driven off the German infantry, who had approached to within thirty yards of the building. Bill Wilson's account of what he found is almost lurid in its detail

Pulling the rather shaken 10 Platoon together, I started to lead them back to their position. We had just got into the tiny yard at the back of HQ when a shell landed in the kitchen doorway. Lance Corporal [Percy] Badnell, one of my signallers, was killed outright, dreadfully mutilated. About ten others were badly injured. Private [William] Phelps next to me had both legs blown off save for tiny threads of muscle. I was, for the third time, amazingly lucky, receiving only a small piece of shrapnel in the thigh.

Discovering the Cheshire machine gunners had abandoned their positions above the farm and had left their weapons behind them, Wilson organised the remnants of 10 Platoon and positioned them in the vacated Cheshire trenches, while he and the stretcher bearers collected the wounded from the farm. At one point in the morning it looked very much as if an armoured attack was about to be launched against them, and Gilmore sent three carriers and the reserve platoon down to them to bolster the company's fire power:

The battle continued past midday. About that time, hearing that PSM Morgan had been wounded and evacuated, I went to see 11 Platoon. Running through the gardens between the whine and whistle of shell and mortar bomb, flinging ourselves flat whenever we heard a near one coming, CSM Robinson and I reached 11 Platoon to find Sergeant Reay in charge and all well in hand.

On the far side of Rue de Watten, D Company were also under attack, reporting shells falling in their positions at the rate of one a minute and that tanks were in evidence at the Croix Rouge fork. Captain Eric Jones and Signaller Smythe from D Company both maintain that PSM William Rumble, commanding 18

Platoon, was killed by shell fire during this action, and not on the previous day, as recorded on the CWGC database.

After directing one section of 140/Field Regiment's guns to the fork in the road near B Company HQ, Gilmore dispatched Second Lieutenant French to liaise with the gunners. Lance Corporal Greenhough describes the events that followed:

> At about midday a British field gun was firing at a copse in front. The Germans engaged them with trench mortars. During the mortar fire I saw 2nd Lieutenant French and PSM Morgan go towards the field gun with the intention of pointing out to its commander the position of the German mortar which they had spotted. When they reached the field gun I saw a mortar bomb score a direct hit on it. I heard PSM Morgan call for water. I took some water to them and found 2nd Lieutenant French had been killed and PSM Morgan wounded in his head and both legs.

The attack was held and gradually the shelling died down, with companies reporting that the enemy had withdrawn from their respective fronts. But from the B Company vantage point large numbers of German troop carriers were seen heading east and crossing the D219 Dunkerque road. During a lull in the shelling, Maurice Gilmore was summoned to Brigade HQ during the afternoon to learn that he had finally been appointed to command the battalion with the rank of Lieutenant Colonel.

During the early part of the morning a badly shaken despatch rider arrived at Somerset's HQ with orders to withdraw, an order which should have arrived the previous day. Apparently Captain John Vaughan, serving with the 8/Worcesters,

An abandoned Bofors gun at Place du Général Vandamme

had spoken to the despatch rider ten miles to the north-east at Bambecque early on the 29 May. Vaughn says the despatch rider was asking the way to Cassel after getting lost during the night. Whether this was because the despatch rider was trying to avoid enemy patrols is unclear, but Vaughan gave the man directions, which explains why the order to withdraw did not reach Somerset until after 8.30am.

With Cassel surrounded, the lateness of the message had effectively landed the whole garrison 'in the bag'. Michael Duncan's grim assessment of the situation did not hide his irritation:

Panzer II tanks of the 6th Panzer Division moving towards Cassel. Note the aerial recognition flags draped across the rear of each vehicle

It was already too late. Even had it been possible to break off the battle, which it was not, no attempt could be made to leave during the hours of daylight, and, by nightfall, all the enemy tank units had been heavily reinforced with infantry, so that the chances of even getting out of Cassel were small whilst those of reaching Dunkerque were hardly worth a consideration.'

The devastation in Place du Général Vandamme after the British withdrawal. Some of 140/Field Regiment's guns can be seen in the foreground with an abandoned gun tractor behind

Nevertheless, orders for the withdrawal were circulated and zero hour set for 9.30pm. The arrival of the despatch rider with the order to withdraw accounts for the East Riding Yeomanry patrol, under Second Lieutenant Nick Wilmot-Smith, that was sent out from Cassel with a composite troop of three tanks. Their task was to patrol the road up as far as Droogland. Somerset was clearly planning the brigade's escape and had fixed his attentions on the D137. Wilmot-Smith's patrol was accompanied by Major Mercer and two anti-tank guns from 211/Battery, who were initially left at the le Temple crossroads with one tank and then brought up to the crossroads at Winnezeele.

The East Riding Yeomanry patrol then continued towards Droogland where Wilmot-Brown's tank was hit by hostile fire, killing his driver and disabling the tank. Managing to return to Winnezeele on foot, he radioed Cassel for assistance, and set out in another tank to stalk the anti-tank gun that had knocked his own tank out. On this occasion his luck ran out, his tank was destroyed again by an anti-tank round and his driver and gunner killed. After abandoning the vehicle he was taken prisoner.

Assistance was dispatched from Cassel in the form of Second Lieutenant Michael Lindley and three further tanks, which left Cassel at 4.30pm with orders to contact Wilmot-Smith and keep the road to Watou open. Lindley's column had a trouble free journey to Winnezeele, where they met Major Mercer's gun crew, and decided to press on towards Herzeele. Corporal Harold Parnaby, commanding one of the tanks, remembered running into a column of German tanks:

The wreckage in the square near the Collégiale Notre-Dame de la Crypte

Our lead tank, commanded by Corporal Rowe, came out of the lane onto the metalled road right in amongst the moving enemy column. He, Corporal Rowe, realised the error of the position and gave the order to his driver – 'tank about' -. The driver pulled the tank around hard to get back on the lane, but finished up with one track in a deep ditch and stuck there. The Germans apparently did not realise what had happened and went on their way. Second Lieutenant Lindley ordered us to dismount, which we did after immobilising the guns and the tanks, and we started to make our way back to Cassel on foot.

Major Joseph Thorne, taken when a lieutenant between the wars

Back at Cassel shellfire continued to harass the garrison and the Gendamerie on Rue de Bergues was hit several times by shellfire. David Wild was in the building at the time and witnessed the death of Major Thorne, the 4/Ox and Bucks' second in command:

The second shot blew off the top corner of our building, whereupon Colonel

German troops inspecting British vehicles in Rue Alexis Bafcop

Place du Général Vandamme pictured after the withdrawal. looking towards Rue St-Nicholas

Kennedy ordered us into the cellar on the south and street side of the building, where the East Riding Yeomanry had their headquarters. As there were over a dozen officers in the room, I sat on the floor near the door exit to Joe Thorn with our backs to the north wall of the cellar. It seemed that a third shell passed clean through the house and did not explode until it struck the wall just where Joe Thorn was sitting. The detonation was terrific and I forced my way to my feet with the wall collapsing round my shoulders ... The two steel girders and all the vaulting had come down, and in the rubble we found Joe Thorne, who by a miracle had been the only fatal casualty.

The garrison assembled between Cassel and the Mont de Récollets and moved off towards Dunkerque in single file, the last unit to leave the stricken town being the East Riding Yeomanry. It is a matter of record that the rearguard actions fought by the East Riding Yeomanry were largely responsible for keeping a large German force occupied while 145 Brigade attempted to reach the coast. The events that followed the withdrawal from Cassel will be looked at further in Chapter 7.

Chapter 4

Hondeghem

The K Battery route from the La Croix Rouge fork may well have taken them through Cassel and onto the D53 through Ste-Marie-Cappel to Hondeghem. Arriving late on 24 May, the battery, with the accompanying troops of 5/Battery, 2/Searchlight Regiment, had ample time to prepare the village for defence. Today, apart from the new private houses that have been built on the outskirts of the village, Hondeghen remains largely as it was in May 1940, with all roads leading to the central square. It was in this square around the church that Rawdon Hoare deployed two of his guns – K and L Subsections – with I and J Subsections covering the southern approaches to the village on Rue de Staple. Headquarters, under Battery Sergeant Major (BSM) Millard, was set up close to the church, while the remaining troops were set to work blocking roads and preparing defensive positions. Two major roadblocks were constructed on the D161, after Rawdon Hoare presumed – quite correctly - that the main threat would approach along that road. By dusk on 26 May, K Battery was as ready as it would ever be to defend the village against *Oberst* Johann von Ravenstein's battle group. Troop Sergeant Major (TSM) Ralph Opie made his rounds at 4.00pm on 27 May to check that all was in place for the coming battle:

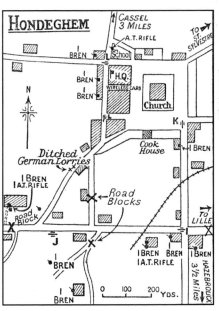

A map of Hondeghem as it appears in Douglas William's account.

I visited all the gun positions in and around the village and found everything present and correct. The whole of the troop Stood To. On completion of my rounds, I returned to the cookhouse in the village, collected the morning 'gun fire' in a 15cwt and proceeded to take it around the gun and Bren gun positions. On finishing, I reported to Captain Teacher that everything was in order.

At 5.00am on 27 May, the German advance towards l'Hazewinde and Poperinghe along the D161 was under the command of *Hauptmann* Eric Löwe, who had with him elements of the 65/Panzer Regiment and the motorised infantry of

IR4. With orders to crush any resistance en-route, the German column reached the roadblock on the D161 at about 8.15am on 27 May, where the leading tanks were fired on by the J Subsection Gun and, possibly, by the I Subsection Gun, which was 700 yards further east on Rue de Staple.TSM Opie was at the J Subsection gun position when he observed the German column break across to the fields on their right and moments later the gun came under attack:

After a wait of about three minutes the first German tank came into sight, it was already firing at an anti-tank rifle situated about 60 yards on out right When the whole of the tank could be seen, I gave the order to fire. The range was approximately 90 yards. The tank was put out of action. Immediately, several enemy tanks appeared and fanned right and left of the road. I gave the orders to engage the right hand tank.

Hauptmann Eric Löwe was killed in Russia in 1943

Still under attack from enemy armoured vehicles and advancing infantry, the J Gun took a direct hit, killing one of the gun crew and wounding 33-year-old Gunner Reginald Manning in the head and chest and TSM Opie in the head:

The leading tank coming up the road now opened up with his machine gun, killing the No.2 with his first burst. Practically at the same time, the gun received a direct hit from a tank. Gunner Manning was very badly wounded around the head and chest; I was wounded in the head and another (either No.5 or 6) was killed.

Opie and the surviving members of the gun crew struggled to keep the gun firing before they were finally overwhelmed and taken prisoner. Gunner Reginald Manning and TSM Opie were sent back to the German casualty clearing station at St Omer, where Manning died of his wounds. There is little detail as to what took place around the I Gun, but we do know from the German account that the gun was hit by a German mortar shell and put out of action almost immediately after Opie's gun was destroyed. The destruction of the two guns allowed *Hauptmann* Löwe to leave the remaining opposition in the village to the infantry of IR4, and continue his advance along the D161 towards Caëstre.

The news of the demise of the guns on the main road would have travelled back to the village very quickly and if the sounds of battle had not already alerted Rawdon Hoare to the presence of the enemy, the arrival of IR 4 would have left him in no doubt. The German report of the battle in the village was recorded by *Leutnant* Kelletat, whose account leaves us in no doubt of the determination demonstrated by the surviving men of F Troop in their defence of the village. Kelletat and his men arrived just as the D Troop guns opened fire on the village from their positions on the Mont des Récollets, their targets being relayed from the observation post in the church tower. Kelletat's account suggests the German infantry were initially pinned down by the weight of fire coming from the British positions:

> *At around 10.00am our vehicles turned off just ahead of the village onto the byway leading to Hondeghem. As we dismounted, heavy artillery fire rained down on our vehicles from the direction of Cassel ...There was shooting from just about every direction as we entered the village ... I remained with my platoon on the left of the road and advanced a bit further through houses and over hedgerows. Then we ran straight into enemy machine-gun and rifle fire lashing through the hedgerows. We could not see the enemy, but he seemed to have his emplacements everywhere. At any rate an advance towards the centre of the village was out of the question.*

Leutnant Kelletat was probably advancing up Rue St Pierre towards the L Gun, which was firing over open sights down the road. In attempting to cross the road he was slightly wounded by a shell hitting the building just behind him. Hoping to outflank the gun, he moved forward again only to be 'lashed by a sheaf of machine guns fire through the hedgerow'. On Douglas William's 1940 map of the fighting, there is a note that German lorries were ditched on Kalverstraet, presumably after being hit by British fire. This may well have occurred after the ambush by British forces near the private house, resplendent with its own moat, where the road bends slightly to the left.

The L Subsection gun had been manhandled from its original position in the north western corner of the square and was now firing from the southwest corner at the advancing German units, who were attempting to make headway. One of the first targets for the gun was the battery cookhouse which had been occupied by the Germans, and who were busy firing a machine gun from the upper story. One round sealed the fate of the cookhouse and the remains of the machine gun is now a prized possession of the battery. German machine-gun fire was now coming from all quarters and the gun crews were constantly changing position:

> *Both K and L Guns were now hotly engaged, firing at the point blank range of one hundred yards using Fuse 1. So close were the Germans that the gun crews were being bombed with hand grenades, but casualties remained small, only one man having been killed and two wounded. Both guns were*

*in very exposed positions but they maintained a fast rate of accurate fire
and every round took effect.*

It is likely that Captain Jimmy Haggas, commanding B Squadron of the Fife
and Forfar Yeomanry, arrived in the village in response to the request for
reinforcements, although he was under the impression that he was to report to the
brigadier! Haggas' account does not allude to any reaction that Major Rawdon
Hoare may have felt about this instant promotion but it must have raised a few
smiles at the time:

*On arrival at Hondeghem we found it occupied by a troop of RHA under
Major Hawdon Hoare. Two guns were in action but the other section had*

Part of Macforce, the men of 5/
Battery, 2/Searchlight Regiment
found themselves fighting at
Hondeghem

been previously knocked out ... I formed a line of men with Bren guns and advanced up some streets in order to clear the village, but found they had withdrawn leaving some dead. I later took out a patrol and sighted a strong force of Germans about 1,000 yards away. This force was composed of heavy tanks and motorised infantry. Two large tanks were also moving down a lane some 300 yards away. Meanwhile the shelling of the village increased.

Although the village was in great danger of being enveloped, an element of impatience was creeping into the German assault that had now been held up for at least seven hours by a relatively small British force. It should be remembered that it was not only the gunners that were defending the village; the role of 5/Battery, 2/Searchlight Regiment is often overlooked and without their supporting fire, it is doubtful that the two remaining guns of K Battery would have been able to stay in action for so long.

Leutnant Kelletat on hearing he was the only officer remaining alive in his *kompanie* reported back to regimental headquarters where he was told brusquely to take command and 'mop up the village'. Returning to his men, he ordered the observation post in the church tower destroyed and prepared for the final attack.

It would have been around this time that Rawdon Hoare decided the moment to withdraw had arrived, particularly as ammunition was low and there appeared to be little hope of reinforcements. Douglas Williams, in his 1940 account, says the withdrawal took place at 4.15pm, when two columns left the village during a lull in enemy activity. The first, containing all the wounded and the two guns, was sent off ahead to rendezvous at St-Sylvestre-Cappel, two miles to the northeast, with the second, which left a short time afterwards, taking a different route.

At St-Sylvestre-Cappel the column ran into units of the 6th Panzer Division, which had already occupied the village. Douglas Williams again:

A volley of hand grenades suddenly started from behind the tombstones in the graveyard. Germans appeared on all sides and the troop commander [Captain Brian Teacher] decided they could only be dislodged by the desperate measure of a direct charge. Two parties armed with rifles and bayonets advanced round

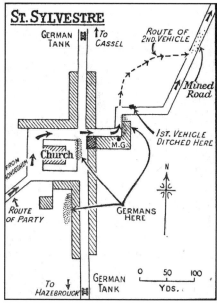

A map of the situation at St Sylvestre Cappel as it appears in Douglas William's account

73

each side of the churchyard wall, each man shouting as he had been ordered to do, at the top of his voice. A terrible roar went up and the psychological effect was immediately apparent. Three or four Germans were shot and the rest, throwing away their rifles, broke into a panic stricken rout.

Despite both guns coming into action again, the writing was on the wall for F Troop as German tanks moved in and destroyed the K Gun, leaving the crew of L Gun to put their own weapon out of action before clambering into the remaining lorries and departing in haste. But the drama was not quite over. One vehicle ended up in a ditch, while another missed a turning and hurtled through a hedge into a field, regaining the road only after smashing through a set of railings. Incredibly, with machine-gun and rifle rounds whistling all around them, most of them got away. However, the final word must go to the startled expressions on the faces of the men of C Squadron East Riding Yeomanry when they learned that F Troop had driven over the very road they had mined with the loss of only one vehicle!

Predictably, the casualty figures for the fight at Hondeghem and St- Sylvestre-Cappel were high. F Troop alone lost forty-five men out of the sixty-three that marched into Hondeghem but the majority would have been wounded as, apart from the two casualties buried at Cassel Communal Cemetery, there are only fifteen men of 5/RHA recorded on the CWGC database who were probably killed with F Troop. To those that survived, the award of the DSO to Major Rawdon Hoare and the MC to Brian Teacher served as an official recognition of the K Battery stand, while the award of the DCM to BSM Reginald Millard and the MM to Gunner Kavanagh, together with the three others mentioned in despatches, was further testimony of the bravery of those who manned the guns and ammunition limbers. Casualties from 5/Battery of 2/Searchlight Regiment are more difficult to find and the CWGC database record only two being killed on 27 May. There is no way of knowing the complete list of German casualties, but at least seven men were killed in *Leutnant* Kelletat's *kompanie*.

Chapter 5

Hazebrouck

Hazebrouck had been a hive of activity since Gort and Pownall had arrived on the afternoon of 22 May with the intention of moving their command post and reuniting GHQ in the town; a move that was swiftly reversed when news of the enemy incursions on the Canal Line dictated a rapid relocation. The message sent to Brigadier Somerset, whilst en-route from Nomain with 145 Brigade, was typical of all military communications - short and very much to the point:

> *Detach one* [battalion] *and two anti-tank batteries from your force in Bailleul. Send them by* [motor transport] *to Strazeele where* [detachment] *will debus and report to Maj Gen Curtis. They will be used as the garrison at Hazebrouck. Col Wood at present OC* [Officer Commanding] *garrison in Hazebrouck will command these troops on arrival.*

Woodforce

On 21 May Woodforce was created at Hazebrouck under the command of Colonel John Wood, Gort's Deputy Director of Artillery, with instructions to defend GHQ at Hazebrouck until relieved. It was to be a very short lived command, lasting a mere four days. The composition of Woodforce appeared to change hourly as troops - largely clerks and orderlies from GHQ (codenamed Brassard) and returning men from leave - were collected and dispersed to the various sectors in the town. However, there was one Belgian unit from the 21st Line Infantry, under Lieutenant Delmonte, who were deployed with their machine guns around the Hazebrouck perimeter; and eighteen French Renault F-17 light tanks, of First World War vintage, which were under French command. The Woodforce Order of Battle also confirms the presence of

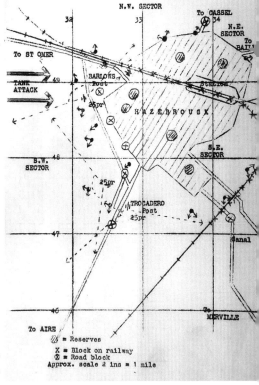

A map of the Woodforce dispositions at Hazebrouck

some two hundred French engineers under the command of *Capitaine* Borelly. Whether these men evacuated the town with GHQ is unknown, but they are not mentioned specifically in the 1/Bucks accounts of the fighting.

Wood organised Hazebrouck's defences around two main posts - Barlow's Post in the northwest and Trocadero Post in the south - both of which operated in conjunction with the four sector garrisons positioned around the town. Each sector had a small local reserve and a mobile reserve was held at GHQ to cover all eventualities.

Throughout the day on 23 May there were various reports of enemy armoured vehicles approaching Hazebrouck from the west and at least one enemy tank was knocked out near Ebblinghem. Clearly concerned at the enemy advances, and the fact that GHQ was coming under attack from the south and west, one gun from 392/Battery, 98/Field Regiment, was stopped as it passed through Hazebrouck en-route for St Omer. They were directed to a garden at les Cinq Rues, just west of Hazebrouck, where the crew dug in to await the arrival of the enemy.

At 9.00am on 24 May – despite the Hitler halt order - observers at Barlow's Post observed enemy tanks from the 8th Panzer Division had crossed the railway line and headed north. Forty minutes later the garrison at Trocadero Post was attacked by eight tanks, reportedly Panzer III and IVs. Barlow's Post came under attack shortly afterwards. In both cases the enemy tanks were checked by fire from 25-pounders. It is not clear whether these guns were from 98/Field Regiment's 391/Battery, or those from the Ordanance Depot at Strazeele. The war diary mentions that Captain E Tremlett and A Troop were in action on the west side of Hazebrouck at 4.00pm on 24 May, which does not equate with the time given in the Woodforce diary, leaving the author to conclude that there were two separate actions.

At les Cinq Rues the 392/Battery gun (E2) and its crew waited patiently until 2.00pm, when German armoured units were seen advancing along the St Omer road:

> [the gun] *opened fire as soon as the column came into sight and her first shot disabled one of the leading vehicles. The enemy halted and withdrew, but not without sustaining several more hits from the gun. After about a quarter of an hour the second round of the engagement was opened by the enemy who brought up eleven medium or heavy tanks to attack the gun ... one tank was put out of action by a direct hit and it is probable that at least two others were badly damaged. But the odds were too heavy.*

Three direct hits were then scored on the gun, the first disabling the layer, whose place was taken by Sergeant Mordin. The second shot wounded Mordin in the eye but he continued operating the gun until the third shell killed Lance Sergeant Godfrey Woolven and badly injured the remaining crew. At this moment the reserve ammunition limber arrived on the scene and was promptly destroyed by another direct hit. With the gun disabled, Mordin ordered a withdrawal.

The Château de l'Orme, which was intended to become Lord Gort's Command Post

GHQ

What remained of GHQ at Arras finally moved to Hazebrouck on 19 May and occupied the Institut St Jacques, which was almost opposite the orphanage on Rue de la Sous-Préfécture. It was intended that Gort's command post would move to the Château de l'Orme, which was immediately south of the Communal Cemetery on Rue de Thérouanne, but events overran the intended move, and it was never made. Brigadier Charles Norman visited GHQ on Rue de la Sous-Préfécture at 3.00am on 23 May:

I found it in the large cellars of a château [sic] *amongst aisles of beautiful arched brickwork. The floors were littered with packing cases of maps and papers, some with their lids off and maps hanging out. The exhausted clerks and orderlies were sleeping among them, some with blankets and some without. Two weary staff officers on night duty were sitting at a trestle table covered with maps. The only light was from a few candles stuck in bottles. It would have made a dramatic stage setting.*

But GHQ was destined to move again within the next forty-eight hours. Their departure on the 24 and 25 May can hardly be described as an orderly one, many documents were left either in the building or at the railway station and some of these were shown to Major Elliot Viney after his capture. The 5/RHA war diary makes mention of Lieutenant General Pownall, Gort's Chief of Staff, arriving at Cassel on 27 May to assess the suitability of the Château Masson as a possible

77

The orphanage on Rue de la Sous-Préfécture where Brian Heyworth based his Battalion Headquarters

location for GHQ. Finding the enemy closing in, GHQ was apparently moved: first to Houtkerque before being finally established in a seaside villa at La Panne (now called De Panne).

1/Buckinghamshire Battalion

Major Brian Kay Heyworth

Commanded by Major Brian Heyworth, who replaced 46-year-old Lieutenant Colonel Alexander Burnett-Brown on 17 May, this Territorial battalion was plunged headlong into a situation at Hazebrouck that would have daunted many of those in the regular army. Arriving in the town at 10.00am on 25 May, the battalion began cooking breakfast in the main street while Heyworth established his Battalion HQ at the orphanage on Rue de la Sous-Préfécture (occasionally referred to in some accounts as the convent). Here the battalion RAP, under Lieutenant Trevor Gibbens, were based, along with Heyworth's Adjudant, Captain James Richie, and Major Elliot Viney, the battalion's second in command. Heyworth quickly realised that, given the number of men under his command, it was all but impossible to defend the whole town. Having made his initial reconnaissance, Heyworth – hoping the railway lines would form a rudimentary anti-tank barrier – deployed his companies to hold that portion of the town that was south of the Calais-Bailleul railway and west of the line running south to Isbergues. North of the railway, the

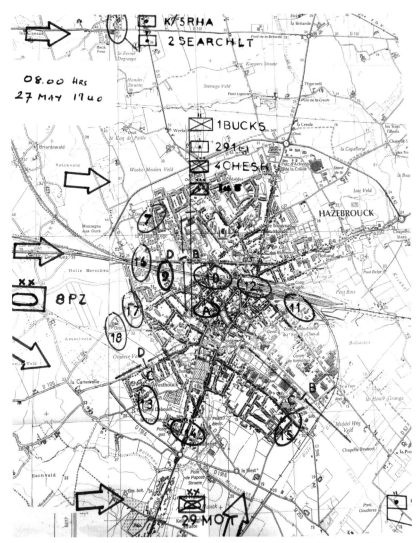

A map of the 1/Bucks dispositions at Hazebrouck, showing Hondegem in the north and the initial assault of the German 8th Panzer Division. Hondeghem and the movement of 65 Panzer Regiment can be seen to the north

gunners from 223/Battery, 56/Anti-Tank Regiment, were deployed to guard the northern approaches to the town.

In the circumstances it was an entirely sensible decision. Even then, there were several undefended gaps between company positions; gaps that Major Elliot Viney worried – correctly as it turned out - would leave the town susceptible to infiltration by German infantry. All the company positions were within walking

The underpass near the station that was defended by a platoon from B Company

distance of Rue de la Sous-Préfécture and, although no mention is made, there must have been telephone lines laid to each company HQ, most of which would have been cut by German shellfire on 27 May.

The battalion was in effect being asked to defend a perimeter seven to eight times longer than would be normally recommended for a battalion at full strength.

It is unlikely that Heyworth could have held out at Hazebrouck as long as he did without the support of the guns of 98/Field Regiment, leaving one to wonder exactly why Major Viney was under the impression that the gunners retired after the first shot was fired. D Company (Captain Hugh Saunders) was deployed in the north western sector of the town, covering the St Omer road, B Company (Captain John Kaye) covered the north and north west, and C Company (Captain Rupert Barry) was positioned in the south and south west, astride the Morbecque road and railway line. A Company (Captain Richard Stevens) was held in reserve at the Institut St Jacques on Rue de la Sous-Préfécture. Captain Cecil Pallett, the battalion quartermaster, and Captain Bligh Mason, the Transport Officer, were based with the A Echelon transport in a linen factory on Rue de Merville.

Captain Rupert Barry commanded C Company

80

226/Field Company, Royal Engineers

No.2 Section, under the command of Second Lieutenant D Keeble, was detached from the main force on 24 May and headed to Hazebrouck with the 1/Bucks. Section HQ was established in St Eloi churchyard and Keeble accompanied Brian Heyworth on his initial reconnaissance of Hazebrouck. Keeble's main priorities were the creation of road blocks and the demolition of bridges over the Hazebrouck Canal. Utilizing some of the abandoned French tanks as road blocks, he also mined several of the approach roads.

98/Field Regiment, Royal Artillery

Commanded by 50-year-old Lieutenant Colonel George Ledingham, the regiment spent much of 25 May reorganising the two batteries commanded by Major Charles Egerton (391/Battery) and Major Hon Charles Cubitt (392/Battery). Major Cubitt's battery had been in action along the Aa Canal, contesting the crossing points from St Momelin to Wittes. (Sergeant Mordin, commanding the E2 Gun at Cinq Rues, had already been evacuated.) The remaining guns and personnel from 392/Battery were cobbled together to form a composite battery of six guns, which was strengthened by the addition of two further 25-pounders and their crews that had been left behind by Woodforce. The war diary states that

One battery of the 98/Field Regiment guns were deployed at le Souverain Farm, southeast of Hazebrouck

F Troop were deployed on the western edge of town north of the St Omer road, and A Troop were positioned south of the road, in the D Company area, with the two left hand guns covering the Morbecque road. Two guns were positioned with the 1/Bucks D Company on the St Omer road and two more were deployed in the southwest of the town between D and C Companies. Two further guns – one of which was found to be out of order - were positioned to cover the open southern approaches from Morbecque.

The second battery – B, C and D Troops forming 391/Battery - and Regimental HQ were located at a farm called Le Souverain, just southeast of Hazebrouck and were on call through Second Lieutenant John Palmer, whose observation post was in St Eloi's church tower.

The ever resourceful Ledingham, who was awarded the MC in 1915 and captained the united services rugby team in 1917, also scrounged two new guns from the Ordnance Depot and, by the time the 1/Bucks arrived at Hazebrouck, the battery at Le Souverain was up to full strength with eight guns. On 24 May Captain Tremlett, commanding A Troop, 391/Battery, was appointed Anti-Tank Commander at Hazebrouck, and it was he who integrated the eight 25-pounders, the 223/Battery 2-pounders and Sergeant Trussel's 25mm Hotchkiss guns into an all round defence. Tremlett appears to have had the approval of Brigadier Somerset and Lieutenant Colonel Durand from 5/RHA, who was acting Chief

The 25mm Hotchkiss anti-tank gun was a French designed weapon and issued to the BEF in 1939. 145 Brigade Anti-Tank Company would have been issued with these guns

Artillery Officer (CRA), as their visit to Hazebrouck at 6.00pm on 26 May makes no mention of the need to reinforce the town's defences or reposition any of the gun crews.

223 Battery, 56/Anti-Tank Regiment

The battery, under the command of Major Ike Pedley, was attached to Macforce on 18 May. The 223/Battery war diary for May 1940 appears to be missing and it is only from indications in other accounts that we can build up a picture of events. The battery was first sent to Cassel with six guns, with another four being deployed along the BEF perimeter. but on 26 May four of these were sent to Hazebrouck to reinforce the battery's guns that were already in the town. I Troop was under the command of Second Lieutenant Dennis Timms and were deployed north of the railway line in the Cité de Cheminots, possibly two of the battery guns were positioned in the south. Sadly, little more precise information on gun positions and their respective crews is currently available.

145 Brigade Anti-Tank Platoon

The Buckinghamshire Platoon at Hazebrouck was commanded by Sergeant Ken Trussel and was armed with 25mm Hotchkiss guns. He and his platoon were placed under the command of Captain Tremlett on 24/25 May. From all accounts Trussel's leadership and example to his men under fire was outstanding.

4/Cheshires

There is no mention in the Cheshires' war diary of a detachment at Hazebrouck but there was a section of Cheshires under Captain Holbrook attached to Woodforce, although it is not clear whether these men were evacuated with GHQ on 24 May. However, a number of sources do refer to the Cheshires' machine guns and, while there is little doubt they were present at Hazebrouck, either having arrived with the 1/Bucks or with Woodforce, their machine guns added crucial fire power to the defending troops.

6/York and Lancaster

The 1/Bucks war diary mentions a returning leave party of 6/York and Lancaster men who were presumably looking for their parent battalion. They were conscripted into A Company and used as part of the battalion reserve but their own battalion war diary makes no mention of them and it is not clear how many managed to get to Dunkerque after Hazebrouck was overwhelmed.

German Armoured Units and Formations

By 24 May XXXXI Panzer Korps under *Generalleutnant* Georg-Hans Reinhardt – 6th and 8th Panzer Divisions and the *SS-Verfügungs* Motorized Infantry Division,

Generalleutnant Adolph-Friedrich Kuntzen

had reached the line of the Aa Canal, where the main force were immobilized by the Hitler halt order. However, on the morning of 24 May an armoured column – most probably a patrol from 8 *Panzer Aufkärungs Abteilung 59* - headed towards Hazebrouck from St Omer and probed the Woodforce defences. The armoured column that came into contact with the single gun from 392/Battery at Cinq Rues was in all probability from the 8th Panzer Division, which had crossed the canal at Blaringhem and approached Hazebrouck from the direction of Lynde.

Generalleutnant Georg-Hans Reinhardt

The 8th Panzer Division, commanded by *Generalleutnant* Adolph-Friedrich Kuntzen, was organized into two battle groups. *Kampfgruppe Oberst* Walter Neumann-Silkow, consisting of a panzer battalion and a battalion of motorized infantry, and *Kampfgruppe Oberstleutnant* Friedrich Sieberg, consisting of a battalion of Skoda PzKpfw 38t tanks, the 59th Panzer Pioneer Battalion (under the leadership of their commanding officer *Oberstleutnant* Karl-Adolph von Bodecker) and a motorized rifle battalion, commanded by *Oberstleutnant*

Oberstleutnant Friedrich-Wilhelm Sieberg

Wilhelm Cristolli. The SS-Verfügungs Division, commanded by *Generalleutnant der Waffen SS* Paul Hausser, became bogged down with the fighting in the Forest of Nieppe, which was held by 132 Brigade, and took little part in the battle for Hazebrouck. The German attack recommenced at 8.00am on 27 May.

Oberst Walter Neumann-Silkow

84

Chapter 6

Let Battle Commence

Hazebrouck had been severely bombed on several occasions prior to the arrival of the 1/Bucks, resulting in the majority of the inhabitants leaving or taking to their cellars. Thus it was a largely deserted town that greeted the 33-year-old Heyworth's preliminary reconnaissance, apart from the *Luftwaffe,* who regularly machine gunned the streets. Despite the highly organised defence of the town under Woodforce, Heyworth had some difficulty in establishing with any accuracy exactly how many troops he was to command and was only furnished with one map, which caused some initial difficulties. Extracting an approximate list from Captain Alistair Campbell, who was in command of the Woodforce troops remaining in the town, he set about examining exactly what he had been ordered to defend.

A map of the 1/Bucks dispositions at Hazebrouck as published in the Regimental Journal in July 1943

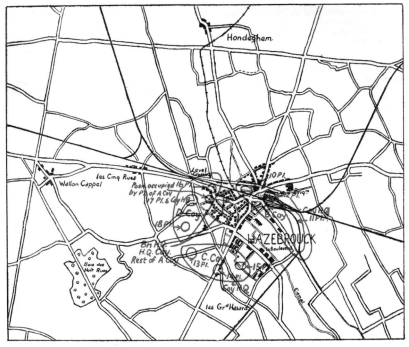

A Cambridge graduate, Heyworth moved from Manchester in 1936 after his appointment as a barrister in the Treasury Solicitor's Department in London; a move that took him to Beaconsfield and a transfer to the Ox and Bucks Light Infantry Depot at Newbury. Ingram Murray suggests that there were indications that Elliot Viney disliked Brian Heyworth 'who he found pedantic' and that 'Viney himself was regarded as arrogant by his juniors'. But whatever feelings passed between the two men – Heyworth was a day junior to Viney - Heyworth was made acting commanding officer, leaving Captain QM Cecil Pallett as the only man in the battalion with any experience of combat.

With three companies in place south of the main railway line and A Company occupying the former GHQ building, the remainder of 25 May was largely spent in completing the take-over from GHQ and in strengthening company defences. Lieutenant Trevor Gibbens, the medical officer attached to the battalion, found the orphanage cellar a convenient location in which to set up the RAP and spent most of the next two days collecting medical supplies from any doctors' houses he could find in the town. Fortunately ambulances were still able to come and go without much enemy interference, as were individuals from other units seeking medical treatment. One of these was a gunner officer from 98/Field Regiment:

A Jeep came roaring up the road and stopped. An officer beside the driver got out and said in the most conversational tone 'I seem to have got one in the elbow, doc'. I cut off his sleeve and realized that his elbow joint had been completely shot away, with a gap of an inch or two between the bones. The radial artery and tissues in the limb were intact, so I put a long wire splint on the whole arm and sent him off in one of the last ambulances.

The individual in question was 30-year-old Captain Lord Cowdray (Weetman John Pearson), who commanded B Troop, 391/Battery. He had been hit northeast of Steenbecque by a burst of machine-gun fire, which had also killed 23-year-old Gunner Ronald Scoates, who was driving Cowdray's vehicle,

Captain Lord Cowdray, 98/Field Regiment, taken after the war

and wounded one of the two signallers in the back. The lead vehicle contained another 98/Field Regiment officer, Major Charles Egerton, the 391/Battery commander, who was killed almost immediately in the same ambush. Cowdray later had his arm amputated but was successfully evacuated from Dunkerque, thanks to Gibbens.

Sunday 26 May

First light saw patrols from A Company sent out along the railway to Morbecque. The *Ox and Bucks War Chronicle* tells us that during the day some two hundred men straggled into the town in an exhausted state. Some of these may have been the leave detail from the 6/York and Lancaster and a few may possibly have been from the 4/Cheshires.

> *All these men were attached to A Company, where they formed one machine gun and three rifle platoons. Most of the men were without rifles and ammunition, the remainder being given hand grenades and axes.*

Quite what they were supposed to do with the axes is anyone's guess! The *Ox and Bucks War Chronicle* also mentions that by 26 May it was 'realised that some form of evacuation was taking place at Dunkerque'. This may have more become more apparent to some of the senior officers of the battalion as they took over from GHQ, but for the bulk of the battalion ignorance remained bliss! Major Viney went so far as to say that 'intelligence rarely filtered down below brigade level' and they learnt more from 'copies of the *Daily Telegraph* than they ever did from higher up'.

Monday 27 May

The battle for Hazebrouck began on a wet and misty morning, when tanks from the 8th Panzer Division overran the 2/Royal Sussex positions south of the town.

SS Graves at Morbecque, where 132 Brigade were fighting the panzer units of the SS-Verfügungs Division

One of the first units in action was the Royal Sussex's D Company, which was overwhelmed by tanks from *Oberst* Neumann-Silkow's Panzer *Kampfgruppe* in the Bois des Huit Rues. Shortly after this the battle opened in Hugh Saunders' sector when his attention was drawn to a German vehicle near the level crossing on the western edge of his sector. Calling in artillery support from a nearby 25-pounder of 392/Battery, he was more than a little peeved when the gunners missed their target, allowing the German reconnaissance group to escape. It was not long before the tanks arrived:

> *We had not been back in our Company HQ for more than a quarter of an hour before three light tanks appeared and swooped down on the 25-pounder, smashing the gun and wounding all its crew save one. The crew retreated through one of 17 Platoon's outposts, hotly pursued by two tanks, which fired a salvo straight into the weapon pits, before they turned and made their way off.*

Saunders was relieved to discover there were no casualties from 17 Platoon; but the ease with which enemy tanks had penetrated the perimeter left no one in any doubt of what was to come. At 10.00am Saunders received a message from Second Lieutenant Tom Garside, commanding 18 Platoon, that a large force of enemy armoured vehicles was approaching from the direction of St Omer, a message confirmed ten minutes later by the observation post on the Wallon-Cappel road. Saunders had a distinct feeling they were 'for it':

German forces approaching Hazebrouck on the Avenue St Omer

> *While we were waiting, for some obscure and still incomprehensible reason, the battalion water truck arrived to fill up eight water bottles which I had reported were empty. The arrival was unhappily the signal for the commencement of the attack and, hardly had [the truck] stopped outside the gate than an enemy tank rushed up from the area of Le Cinq Rues and, with a carefully aimed shot, hit the water cart straight in the [water] tank ... The [German] tank in question was one of three that were circling round 17 Platoon's position, harassing them as much as possible and trying to unnerve the defenders. They were hotly engaged by 17 Platoon's anti-tank rifles and, after one of them was hit, they withdrew.*

98/Field Regiment

By 11.00am all three companies were engaged as enemy tanks probed their defences and German artillery and mortars bombarded their positions, making life very difficult for Lieutenant John Palmer in his observation post in the church tower and eventually forcing him to beat a hasty retreat. The church of St Eloi, built in 1494, is one of the oldest buildings in the town and offered an all round view to the 98/Field Regiment observation post. But Palmer was not to be deterred and by 9.40am he was back in the tower, where he remained for the next six hours. The war diary rather jubilantly commenting that, 'many targets were successfully engaged, including concentrations of tanks and an infantry HQ, both of which were dispersed.' At around 3.40pm the telephone line to le Souverain was finally

The church of St Eloi at Hazebrouck

cut, and the observation post closed down. The, by now badly damaged, church tower was not replaced until 1994. The gunners did not finally withdraw from Hazebrouck until ordered to do so at 9.00pm by Captain Tremlett, by which time the situation had deteriorated significantly and the guns could do no more. At Souverain, the guns remained in situ until 7.00pm, when enemy shelling from the high ground round Morbecque resulted in losses to both men and vehicles.

Attacks on D and C Company

Back in Hazebrouck on the D Company front, a runner from 16 Platoon announced that infantry were being brought up along the St Omer road in strength and although they had already been engaged by Corporal Wade and his section from 17 Platoon, and temporarily scattered by the battalion's single 3-inch mortar, D Company's supremacy over the enemy was short lived. Within minutes a steady machine-gun fire made it almost impossible for anyone to lift their heads. But, as Saunders reflected later, it looked as if the attack was developing in the C Company area.

He was quite correct. While D Company were coming under heavy fire, 30-year-old Captain Rupert Barry and his platoons of C Company were fending off an attack by five enemy tanks with their Boys rifles. Barry was the only regular officer in the battalion, having been transferred from the 2/Ox and Bucks in April. His appointment was considered to be a great asset to the battalion, and his defence at Hazebrouck was certainly one that engendered a magnificent fighting spirit amongst his men.

But it was a desperate fight and, despite putting most of the tanks out of action, 14 Platoon was overrun and another – possibly Lieutenant Geoffrey Rowe's 13 Platoon – was cut off and surrounded by the afternoon. On the A2 Subsection

The Trocadero Tower before it was demolished

gun at the Trocadero, Lance Sergeant Artificer Gordon Hatcher was awarded the MM for his part in the action. Another gunner, - whose name frustratingly eludes the author – disabled his gun late in the afternoon just before it was overrun and was also awarded the MM.

Responding to Barry's SOS, Heyworth ordered A Company to establish a fresh line in the buildings behind C Company in order for Barry and his men to withdraw. Despite Captain Pallet and the Transport Officer forming a defensive line behind C Company with the B Echelon drivers, very few of A Company reached the new line. Sergeant Leslie Phipps was with Barry when the company received orders to withdraw to the new positions:

> *Captain Barry and I set off to sort a new position. It was not, however, to be. We had only crossed the road immediately outside our* [company] *HQ, it ran left to right and we were going at right angles to it, and gone about 50 yards, when an almighty 'Schemozzel' broke out about 75 yards to our left. It was a body of Germans who were shouting and making a tremendous din, presumably to give themselves Dutch Courage. They, as did we, hit the deck and opened fire with machine guns, firing tracer bullets and mortars down the road we had just crossed ... all this fire was, of course, between us and our HQ so we were completely cut off from them.*

Private George Davies was a C Company man, but it appears from his account that he was with Captain Pallet and the A Echelon transport at the linen factory on Rue de Merville. He writes that he had a close encounter with a sniper's bullet at the factory gate 'where the QM and cooks' were busy preparing food. 'I was leaning against the wooden gatepost when a bullet buried itself in the post one

90

inch from my ear'. Whether or not Davies left Hazebrouck with Pallet is not mentioned; but he did manage to get home to England.

B Company

On the eastern edge of the perimeter, Lieutenant Clive Le Neve Foster's 11 Platoon did not have to wait long before it too became engaged by German infantry advancing down the railway line. Beating off the initial attack, the company held their ground under enemy machine-gun fire and occasional sniping, which appeared to be directed from buildings to the north of the railway.

Foster remembered that later that day an anti-tank officer [this may have been Major Ike Pedley] arrived at their positions with news that the Germans were in the north of the town and asking for help in retrieving an anti-tank gun which was 'on the wrong side' of the railway line:

> There was very heavy machine-gun fire down the railway and six sets of rails to get it over. I took the sergeant major and about 8 others for the job and we ran over and all crossed safely. We got hold of the gun and it was a heavy affair to move. We then drove a 15cwt lorry over and after some difficulty hitched it up and got safely back again. I can well remember watching the machine-gun tracer bullets streaking down the line.

Back across the railway line, Foster found that his company had withdrawn and large numbers of German infantry were approaching the town. Quite where the company had gone, and at what time they withdrew, is not clear, but the company commander, Captain John Kaye, and a number of his company were amongst those who made it back to England.

B Company were deployed in and around the railway station covering the northern sector of the town

Saunders and his men in D Company were also conscious that enemy forces were pouring into the town and that they were powerless to stop them:

> *By about 7.00pm the enemy were well inside the town and we could hear the sound of firing in the streets. In several places fires had broken out from incendiary shells and clouds of smoke filled the air, but Battalion HQ was still intact. I decided to make contact, if I possibly could, and Pte Page volunteered to make his way to Battalion HQ. He had only, however, to put his foot outside the gap in the wall which we used as a door to bring a veritable hail of tracer bullets down on him. After several attempts we realized it was hopeless to get out of the building by daylight, as all our lines of departure were covered by machine guns.*

Rue de la Sous-Préfécture

At battalion headquarters the 27-year-old Gibbens was struggling desperately with the wounded as the upper floors of the orphanage were being bombarded by mortars and tank shells. From below floor level they could hear the crack and rumble of masonry as battle raged above:

> *Bit by bit the wounded were brought down ... There was clearly not going to be much opportunity to get the wounded away for some days ... I did the rounds in quiet moments, gave plenty of morphia and sips of water ... one man was brought down with his abdomen completely opened up and his*

The orphanage on Rue de la Sous-Préfécture after the building had been destroyed by German shellfire

The orphanage remained a shell until it was rebuilt after the war

bowels pouring out. There seemed to be nothing to do but put wet, warm packs on him and fill him up with morphia. He died quietly the next day.

Unbeknown to Gibbens, enemy forces were closing on battalion headquarters from three sides, having cut off and surrounded the rifle companies, whose resistance had been reduced to platoon-sized pockets. The battalion had been practically destroyed by the time darkness had descended over a burning Hazebrouck. It appears that in the confusion of battle, withdrawal orders were not received by the men in isolated company positions, and those that did receive them were given no point of reference to withdraw to.

At 8.30pm the Germans completely broke through the D and C Company positions and pushed on towards the centre of town, Saunders took it upon himself to order the surviving men of his company to get away, feeling that in the circumstances Major Heyworth would have acted in a similar fashion. It was a different story for the men still holding out at battalion headquarters. Private Perkins, one of the D Company runners, was one of a number of men who had drifted back to the orphanage, where he was ordered to take up a defensive position:

At two points in the building were Bren guns covering two streets and one more covering the big yard at the back of the building ... Myself, along with the other HQ personnel, took up our positions with our rifles at every available window there was ... for the first hour or two it was more or less a sniper's job, as I had quite a few crack shots at motor cyclists who kept crossing quite frequently at the top [of the road]. The building was now getting in a bad way, one part of it had already collapsed, as at this stage

93

we were handicapped by our anti-tank rifles having been put out of action so it was left to our Bren guns to try and stop the tanks. It was hopeless and heartbreaking for the Bren gunners, their bullets just bounced off, but undaunted they kept on.

The war diary, which was completed by Saunders shortly after he had returned to England, describes the fighting coming to an end around 9.30pm on 27 May. Certainly by nightfall all contact had been lost with the rifle companies and battalion headquarters was surrounded. In a final effort to make contact with any troops still holding on Heyworth sent out two patrols: one to find the B Echelon transport and the other to B Company. Second Lieutenant Martin Preston got as far as Place du Général de Gaulle before he was killed, while Second Lieutenant David Stebbings, the Intelligence Officer, finding the B Company positions deserted, managed to return with the news. Only then was it fully realized at battalion headquarters that 'it and HQ Company were the only parts of the battalion available and capable of fighting another day'.

Monday 28 May

As soon as it was light enemy mortars ranged in on the orphanage, hitting an unloaded ammunition lorry, which added to the noise of battle by a series of continuous explosions for almost two hours. At 1.00pm a number of tanks came past the front of the building firing at almost point blank range at the beleaguered garrison which replied with rifle, anti-tank rifle and Bren gun fire, the intensity of which was reduced somewhat by the GHQ troops' unfamiliarity with the workings of the Lee Enfield rifle! However, the remnants of the battalion continued to

Hazebrouck was overwhelmed by the might of the 8th Panzer Division, although armoured vehicles such as this Panzer IV, were at a disadvantage in built up areas

Renault F-17 Tanks abandoned in the Place du Général de Gaulle at Hazebrouck. These ancient vehicles had been attached to Woodforce

fight back. RSM Albert Hawtin is recorded in Private George Davies' account as disposing of one tank by dropping a grenade into its open turret from one of the upper floors of a building. But the conclusion of the battle was drawing ever closer, something which must have been obvious to all concerned.

The *Ox and Bucks War Chronicle* gives the time of Major Heyworth's death as 4.30pm. He was crossing Rue de la Sous-Préfécture to the former GHQ Headquarters when he was hit by a sniper's bullet. It was an imperfect end to a gallant individual's short life. There is some evidence to suggest Heyworth and Elliott Viney disagreed about surrendering, Heyworth being determined to defend the building to the last man, as he had been ordered. In the author's opinion, the award of the DSO to Major Elliot Viney was made to the wrong man. There is little doubt that if a DSO was warranted, then the recipient of the award should have been Brian Heyworth. But with Heyworth's death, command devolved to Viney, who soon afterwards evacuated the building with the hundred or so men who were still able to fight, taking up position in the small, walled orphanage garden.

It was around this time that the adjutant, 32-year-old Captain James Ritchie, was killed attempting to leave the building by another entrance. Trevor Gibbens' account provides a glimpse of the final minutes before the building collapsed:

The school was virtually being razed to the ground it seemed. The noise of falling floors got louder. I remember hearing that the part of a house which is last to collapse is the doorways. I think it is certainly true. Anyway I stood in the doorway between cellars three and four. Number four led to the stairs to the front door. Soon after the roof came in, covering all the fifty or so wounded on stretchers on the floor with rubble. I imagined they would all be killed and as I walked to the doorway, I remember a voice under the rubble saying "get off my face".

Trapped and with virtually no ammunition, Viney's men waited patiently in the orphanage garden, determined to make their break for freedom under the cover of darkness. It never happened. Spotted by a German patrol, Viney had little choice but to surrender the remaining garrison. The defence of Hazebrouck was over.

Chapter 7

Breakout

When 28-year-old Sergeant Leslie Phipps heard his battalion was to hold Hazebrouck to the last man and last round, he was not altogether happy about the prospect. 'Now this sounds very well on television (not that there was television in those days) or in a John Wayne film, or even in a book', he wrote, 'but it isn't very clever to be actually faced with such a situation.' Six miles northwest of Hazebrouck at Cassel, Second Lieutenant Julian Fane was quite surprised to receive the order to withdraw, particularly after coming to terms with the idea of fighting to the last man:

> We had been ordered to hold Cassel to the last round and the last man to cover the withdrawal to Dunkerque, so we did not expect the order to withdraw. By this time the Germans were all around us and we were prepared to settle down to a good fight. Imagine our surprise when we received the message to break for it if we could.

The difference in age between the two men was almost ten years and, while both would have fought to the last round as ordered, they must have been aware that orders such as these were often rescinded, as they had been on a number of occasions over the past ten days. Nevertheless, Phipps' reaction to the order must have been one that many of the defenders at Cassel and Hazebrouck shared.

Just before 8.00pm Captain Bill Wilson recalled receiving an order to send an officer to Battalion HQ. He sent Lieutenant Richard Olive, who had been suffering from dysentery over the previous few days 'and was completely exhausted' but, as he says in his account, he knew what Gilmore's summons meant, 'in all probability orders for withdrawal':

> He returned with the expected orders – though very vague ones ... Later the written orders came out. We were to withdraw via Watou to Roesbrugge (to cross the Yser) and thence to Hondschoote (to cross the canal). So to make our way to Moëres church ... By 9.30pm our thinning out was complete and we were marching through Cassel in the dark. In the far north Dunkirk still burned and all around were other fires in towns and villages. On the Mont des Récollets we stopped and for some obscure reason took up a meaningless defence position, whilst other troops, Ox and Bucks, REs, gunners etc marched through us and assembled ahead. There we remained until midnight.

Leaving some 200 wounded with 143/Field Ambulance and in the various regimental RAPs, the break-out from Cassel was remarkably successful but, as one might expect, there were casualties as the respective groups came into contact with the surrounding German infantry, and very few men reached the beaches at Dunkerque. Quite why the bulk of 145 Brigade did not leave until after midnight – two and a half hours after they had withdrawn from their positions – is still, for the most part, unexplained. Given that the hours of darkness were their most effective cloak against capture, it does appear their chances of reaching Dunkerque were considerably reduced by the lateness of their departure.

David Wild was with Brigadier Nigel Somerset and remembered a very unpleasant march where everyone bunched up as they moved through hedgerows and clambered over fences:

> Twice we had to make a small detour to avoid going too close to blazing farmhouses. At length we struck a road and followed it for several hundred yards until a burst of machine gun fire ahead drove us into the cover of some houses. After a few minutes the brigadier led us at the double across a road and into a field. At the far side we had to clamber laboriously through a double apron barbed wire fence ... In a corner of a copse I saw a scuffle and Geoffrey Wilkes emerged marching two Germans ahead of him at the point of his pistol. They were part of a tank crew and had been surprised whilst taking a nap ... in the early morning light [of 30 May] a burst of Tommy-gun fire came from behind the hedge, the Germans behind the hedge could not really see where we were and continued firing until our two prisoners, by shouting, induced them to stop.

Wild then found himself in a ditch with Major Griffiths of 226/Field Company, the brigade signals officer and about eighteen men, cooks, drivers and typists, most of whom had never fired a shot. Wet and cold, they discussed the possibility of lying up and pushing on towards Dunkerque that night; but with such a large number of men, their chances of remaining undetected were reduced as daylight finally revealed their presence to the Germans. After a brief consultation, Griffiths walked out across the field, waving his handkerchief in surrender:

> Having stripped our men of their arms, the Germans escorted us to an orchard, where we found the brigadier and his staff already prisoners. As we heard later, those killed in the 4th Battalion were, Jimmy Graham, Godfrey Wykeham, Bertie Falkiner, Joe Pearman-Smith, Colin Dillwyn, Noel Ruck-Nightingale, CSM Bailey and Charlie Clerke Brown, who was highly commended for his work that night by Colonel Thompson of the East Riding Yeomanry, to whom Charlie was attached with his carriers. Colonel Kennedy and Michael Fleming were both wounded.

The 24-year-old Clerke Brown, commanding the Ox and Bucks Carrier Platoon, clashed early on with enemy tanks and died of wounds a week later and Major James Graham, commanding C Company, was killed leading a bayonet charge at Winnezeele. The 38-year-old Graham was a former international athlete and cricketer. Captain Michael Fleming was mortally wounded near Watou and, like Clerke Brown, died of wounds in captivity. CSM Bailey from A Company – although already wounded - was killed while leading an attack on a machine gun post. The 145 Brigade war diary notes that only two officers, one of whom was Captain Brasington, and eight men from the battalion reached the coast.

Lieutenant Michael Duncan was relatively lucky in that, during the night, the party that he was with only bumped into one machine gun post, which accounted for two of his men. However, as dawn broke they found themselves surrounded by a large German column of all arms, including armoured vehicles:

The battle which followed was sharp but could only have one end. We were caught in the open, we had no defence whatever against tanks or armoured vehicles of any kind and we had not slept for twenty-four hours. Such ammunition that we had we fired and, when it was finished, we waited for the enemy to collect us.

With the Ox and Bucks were the men of 100/Field Company. Near Watou the second in command, Captain Deacon, and the interpreter Jean Streichenberges, were wounded and captured; but Major Whitehead managed to evade the encircling Germans, remaining at large for the next eight weeks until he and two others were captured north of Rouen. Lieutenant Mercer and his group were in sight of Dunkirk when they were finally surrounded after crossing an airfield. Prisoner of War statistics indicate the greater part of Major Whitehead's company were killed or taken prisoner.

The surviving Gloucesters began their breakout led by their commanding officer, Lieutenant Colonel Gilmore. At first all went well, but after they had skirted the village of Winnezeele and passed Bois St-Acaire, the presence of German armoured units and accompanying infantry brought them to a halt. Calling his company commanders together, Gilmore ordered a return to the Bois St-Acaire :

The situation was not a pleasant one, for all the men were worn out from lack of sleep and food, and morale was low as was only to be expected in such circumstances. Our route to the sea was cut off and we were an isolated unit completely surrounded by Germans. At the same time it was rapidly growing lighter and the morning mist, our main camouflage, was dispersing ... The CO and HQ Company went forward and must have been captured. We – B, C and D Companies – went into the wood ... but we must have been spotted by the Hun for we had not been there long before the whole area around the wood resounded with the cries of Kamerad! Kamerad! ... It was a nasty moment for us, for we realized the hopeless position we were in – one false move and we would all be shelled to hell.

It was at this point that Fane and a group of other officers and men decided that their only chance lay in finding another position, their dash across open ground

Second Lieutenant Julian Fane

to a nearby wooded area was accompanied by a withering machine gun fire, which accounted for several of the party. Signaller Smythe thinks only about ten men reached the copse. Captain Bill Wilson and the remainder of B Company remained in the larger wood, where they were later captured. Arriving unscathed, and apparently undetected, Fane and his group lay up for the remaining part of the day, only to walk into an ambush that night after they had left the cover of the wood:

[Lieutenant Richard] *Olive, who was just in front of me, got a burst of machine gun fire in the chest. He only lived two minutes after he was hit. CQMS* [Edward] *Farmer, also next to me, got a burst of tracer in the back which set off the rounds he was carrying in a bandolier over his shoulder ... I was just beginning to wonder why I had not been hit when a bomb burst just in front of my head. I was knocked a bit silly by a piece of shrapnel which ricocheted off my tin helmet, and my right shoulder and arm felt exceptionally numb, but soon a warm trickle down my sleeve showed me I had been hit.*

Against all odds, Fane survived this encounter and, accompanied by Sergeant White, scrambled into a nearby ditch, where he teamed up with Corporal Eldridge. Sharing the ditch was Lance Corporal Greenhough and several men from 10 and 11 Platoons, all desperately trying to avoid the German machine gun fire. White was hit some moments later and presumably left behind as, the by now, small group, escaped the German fire and made their way towards Oost Cappel:

We marched all that night [30/31 May]*, working round the flank of the enemy position. Two men could not keep up, so we left them behind, leaving 12 of us in the party. I was without maps or compass. All I had was a revolver and 12 rounds. Eldridge had two grenades and the remainder had about 5 rifles between them. We were a motley crew. There was one man from the 4th Bucks, one RASC and the rest were Gloucesters.*

Signaller Smythe remembered seeing a German convoy of at least fifty troop carriers pass them, 'the Germans seemed to be all round us and they were using searchlights and stationary illuminating lights in the sky'. Eventually, after two further close encounters with the enemy, Fane and his party arrived at Dunkerque on 2 June, and was one of only two officers and eight men to reach the coast.

Another individual who evaded capture was Driver William Martin from

140/Field Regiment. The former butcher, from Kingsbridge in Devon, was with Major Edward Milton's party after leaving Cassel on 29 May. Travelling across country they were eventually surrounded by German tanks, where Milton was wounded and died a short time afterwards. Martin was taken prisoner and marched to Cambrai, where he was put on a train bound for Germany. Escaping from the train, he was recaptured at Hirson, from where he escaped again, only to be recaptured once more near Epernay. Finally, he got away for a third time by scrambling over a wall and in due course made his way to Marseilles and home.

But there was not a happy ending for Major Ronnie Cartland. Before leaving their positions, in Cassel, Cartland called his men together and explained the situation facing them. Harry Munn remembered the occasion well, as Lieutenant Harold Freeker, the battery captain, gave each man cigarettes and a tin of corned beef:

No mention was made that the evacuation was already taking place at Dunkerque. He also said it was 'an every man for himself' situation and that any man who wished to make his own way was free to do so. All elected to follow the major and armed with rifles, Brens and Mills bombs, we set off through the burning town of Cassel ... At dawn we found ourselves under heavy fire from infantry and tanks. Very heavy casualties were inflicted on out battery and to save further losses, Major Cartland gave the order to surrender. At this point heavy firing was going on and Major Cartland was killed. Mr Hutton-Squire, Tommy Bunn, who was the major's driver, and myself were some distance from the rest of the battery. Mr Hutton-Square said he was not going to become a prisoner and shouting 'follow me Bombardier' stormed out of the ditch we were in, and firing a Bren gun at a nearby tank, was killed by the answering burst of fire.

Munn and Tommy Bunn managed to reach a ditch on the far side of the field but after running through a gateway were taken prisoner by a German patrol.

The last unit to leave Cassel was the East Riding Yeomanry, who had destroyed most of their vehicles save one or two tanks and their carriers. In June it was apparent that only seven officers and 230 men of the regiment had got home, a large proportion of which were from the B Echelon detachment, commanded by Second Lieutenant Edmund Scott, who had left Cassel on 28 May. For the remainder, together with the remaining carriers from the Ox and Bucks and Gloucesters, their route lay along the road previously reconnoitred by Lieutenant Wilmot-Smith:

As daylight broke and the mist cleared away, the forward part of the Yeomanry reached Winnezeele and were approaching Droogland when there started up a continuous anti-tank barrage, supported by tanks. Two of the carrier troops were sent forward to see if they could push through, but were destroyed ... Part of A Squadron was sent out on a reconnaissance, but no way through could be found. They were completely outnumbered and appeared to be totally surrounded ... Separated from the remainder of the column and suffering heavy casualties, they advanced across country in a north westerly direction until the carriers in which Second Lieutenant [Norman] Bonner was travelling was hit about 6.00am. He, Captain [Donald] Hall and the crew, walked along ditches before coming across one of the infantry's deserted carriers.

The memorial to the 1/East Riding Yeomanry at Beverly Minster, East Yorkshire

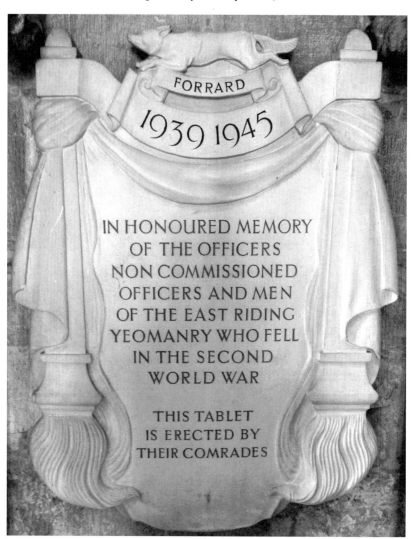

Some of the 1/ERY officers captured in 1940, taken at Oflag VIIC. Standing from left to right: Lt C Bonner, Capt R Smith, Major H Wright, Lt Col W Thompson, Maj J Hodgson, Maj G Wade and Capt (Adjutant) S Bearne.

Unbelievably the carrier started up and they joined 20-year-old Second Lieutenant John Cockin's column as they moved to a wood near Watou. At 6.30am on 30 May they attempted to follow Major Geoffrey Radcliffe towards Houtkerque, but lost him at a crossroads and soon afterwards ran into anti-tank fire, which destroyed the carrier. Finding refuge in a ditch, they crawled along its muddy floor until they ran into enemy troops yet again; in the ensuing fire fight 29-year-old Donald Hall was killed and Bonner wounded. As for Major Radcliffe, he was last seen heading into the woods near Watou.

John Cockin and Second John Lieutenant Dixon actually reached the outskirts of Watou with their troops, but the leading two carriers were hit by anti-tank fire and Cockin was killed, sharing the fate of his elder brother, Phillip, who had been killed serving with A Squadron on 18 May. Phillip is commemorated on the Dunkirk Memorial. Dixon's carrier fared little better, plunging into a steep ditch, he and his driver, Trooper Chris Dodsworth, were thrown into the middle of the road and taken prisoner. As Dixon said himself,

An article printed in the Beverly Observer reporting the reunion dinner of the 1/ERY prisoners of war

THEY FOUGHT IN 1940

E.R. Yeomanry Reunion

There was a happy reunion at the City Restaurant last night of men of the East Riding Yeomanry who served with the regiment in France and Belgium in 1940. Of the 120 officers and men who were present many had spent long terms in prisoners of war camps, some were on leave from the B.L.A., and a few were now serving in other units.

Informality was the order of the evening, but Col. W. D. B. Thompson, D.S.O., M.C., who commanded a battalion up to the time he was taken prisoner at Dunkirk, took advantage of the opportunity to tell them how pleased he was to be among them once again. He said he had spoken to the corps commander who had been in charge of the 1940 operations, and he had said the regiment had done splendid work in the campaign which preceded Dunkirk. They were all proud of the distinguished part the regiment had taken in the D-Day and Rhine crossing operations.

Officers supporting Col. Thompson included Major M. Wright, Major G. Wade, Capt. Mulchinock, Lt. H. J. A. Hopper, and Lt. Bryan Reid.

it was a humiliating end to their escapade. Gradually the remaining parties of the East Riding Yeomanry were mopped up as the noose tightened around the column. A few managed to reach Dunkerque but Lieutenant Colonel Thompson and most of the remaining officers were taken prisoner, and the regiment all but ceased to be a fighting force by 30 May.

By comparison the breakout at Hazebrouck was a far more disorganized and haphazard affair, with the outlying rifle companies taking it upon themselves to withdraw on 27 May; leaving Brian Heyworth and those of his battalion still in the centre of town to fight on. To be fair, all communication between Regimental HQ and the respective company HQs had almost completely broken down and, as the perimeter was slowly overwhelmed, company commanders took it upon themselves to order their men to make for Dunkerque. As to how many of the battalion avoided captivity is uncertain, but official figures suggest ten officers and around 250 other ranks became prisoners of war. Ian Watson, in his study of the 1/Bucks at Hazebrouck, is of the opinion that up to half of the battalion may have escaped, particularly those from the outlying rifle companies.

The question as to why Brian Heyworth and the survivors at the orphanage, took the decision to remain in situ on the night of 27 May remains to a large extent unanswered. Ingram Smith believes the answer lies with Heyworth's determination of character; he had been given orders to hold Hazebrouck to the last man and last round, and as far as he was able that is exactly what he intended to do. An admirable attitude but in the circumstances a little foolhardy.

Captain Hugh Saunders states in his account that it was 10.30 pm on 27 May when he called a conference in the cellar of his D Company HQ and told his men that they were to make their way to the British lines in parties of six or seven:

The first party was to start at 11.15pm; the others to follow at 20 minute intervals. The leader of the parties, in addition to [Second Lieutenant Powell, CSM Badrick and Sergeant Print] *were Cpl Abbot and Cpl Youens, and I directed that the most junior should start first in order that he might have the longer period of darkness in which to move ... It was not easy in the darkness and confusion of the building for parties to find one another but by 12.00 midnight 5 parties had gone and no sound of fire indicated they had been observed. I waited with the 6 men who remained in the building for the 20 minutes to elapse before I should start out. All was quiet as I led my men down the garden out into the fields to begin our long trek which was to finally bring us to Dunkerque.*

With German units penetrating the C Company defences, Captain Barry and Sergeant Phipps were unable to return to their HQ on Rue du Biest. Phipps does not say what time this occurred, but it was after dark that Barry split his remaining troops into small groups under the command of an NCO and sent them off in the direction of Calais – Calais had in fact fallen on the previous day! Leslie Phipps remained with Barry and, with the eight or ten men in the party, made their way to a 'large château' where they found refuge in the stables:

It wasn't very long before some German officers arrived at the back door, which we could see, of the château. They were sorting out which officers would be billeted there, and they wrote in chalk, the details on the door. Soon afterwards we saw that C Company's pick–up truck [Barry's Personal vehicle] had arrived just by the château. As it contained all the rest of Captain Barry's and my gear, great coats etc, and a large cheese we had liberated somewhere along the way, it was all very frustrating.

During the day more German troops arrived and occupied the stable area below the loft where the British were hiding and before long a curious German soldier discovered the presence of Captain Barry's party. Ushered down the ladder at gunpoint, the group marched into captivity.

Second Lieutenant Clive le Neve Foster, who was cut off from B Company, lay up behind the railway embankment with two others until dark, when all three managed to slip away after dark, but not before they stumbled across a German sentry on the railway embankment above then:

I had no map of the district and the first question to decide was which way to go. We decided we should try east, which seemed the most likely direction ... It was just at this time that I looked up and saw a German sentry sauntering along the top of the embankment with his rifle slung over his shoulder. I got my rifle and took careful aim, as well as I could in the dark, and had a shot. It missed, and he just turned round and look rather surprised. I had another shot and missed again. It seemed incredible, and I wondered what would happen next. One of my men then had a shot which knocked him out.

Realising the noise of their encounter would have alerted any nearby German units, the group made off a quickly as they could. After coming across another group of Germans, they crouched down in the darkness, holding their breath until they had passed by, and sometime afterwards they were picked up by a British truck. On reaching British lines they met Second Lieutenant Michael Sherwell and Captain QM Pallet and together the party made their way to Dunkerque via Armentières. On the beach they found Captain Hugh Saunders and a small group of men from D Company:

Our Quarter Master Pallet, who was really the senior officer of the party, was nearly done. He had been through the whole of the last war in the ranks and was about 50 years of age. He told me he thought this was much worse than the last lot ... After we had been on the beach some time, I ran into another officer of our battalion, Captain Saunders, and we were very glad to see each other. He told me he had taken his men on foot across country more or less on a compass bearing.

105

The Military Cross citation for Cecil Pallett and Michael Sherwell

MILITARY CROSS

SHEWELL, Second Lieutenant Michael Geoffrey, Oxf. and Bucks L.I.

At Hazebrook. Second Lieutenant Shewell's platoon occupied a position in houses on either side of a street. Enemy snipers with machine-guns covered the exits from the houses, and the line of withdrawal down into the street. At great personal risk, Second Lieutenant Shewell fearlessly went into the street and shot down several of the snipers. He then led his men out of the town to the village of La Motte.

DIXON, Second Lieutenant Thomas Hugh Peter, R.A.

On May 30 this officer was observed at a burning car dump 800 yards south of Pont-Des Cerps, the only bridge not blown on the Bergues Canal. He was seen to be urgently seeking some form of transport remaining undamaged, and having found an Austin 8, he replied to inquiries that he was going immediately into Hondschoote, about three miles farther south, to collect his senior officer, whom he knew to be wounded. He was warned that this was seemingly impossible as there had been a tank engagement there the previous night and the village was in enemy hands. He said he was aware of it, but that he still intended to go.. It was obvious that odds were heavily against his returning at all—but within 40mins. he returned with a lorry with his senior officer and seven other ranks all wounded.

PALLETT, Captain (Quartermaster) Cecil Alfred, Oxf. and Bucks L.I.

On May 28 Captain Pallett took up a position in the village of La Motte covering the withdrawal of other troops. Quite undaunted by the fact that troops on either side of him had withdrawn, he stayed until he was practically surrounded, and then withdrew in face of the enemy and under fire. He reorganized his men just outside the village, led an immediate counter-attack, and drove the enemy out of the village over or into the canal.

What Pallet and Sherwell may have omitted to mention was that after C Company was overrun, they had made their way south to La Motte au Bois and joined up with the Royal West Kents. On 28 May Pallet led a bayonet charge that pushed the advancing SS Infantry out of the village, enabling their escape and eventual arrival at Dunkerque. Michael Sherwell, who commanded 7 Platoon in A Company, not only managed to guide his men out of their position in the northwest of the town, but also evaded captivity after being sent to reinforce C Company. It was after the demise of C Company that he met up with Pallet. Both men were awarded the MC.

Of the remaining officers and men little is known. Second Lieutenant Sandy Powell from D Company was at large for twelve days before his capture, as was Second Lieutenant John Viccars, who commanded the carrier platoon. Sadly, CSM Badrick was rounded up on the Dunkerque perimeter – almost in sight of the sea.

Chapter 8

The Tours

This section contains the usual advice to visitors and offers the battlefield tourist a general orientation car tour of the Cassel area, involving the actions at le Peckel, Zuytpeene and Bavinchove, before heading south-east to visit Hondeghem and St-Sylvestre-Cappel. In addition there are two walking tours of Cassel that explore the battlefield in greater detail. In order to visit all the company locations, it is recommended the tour of Hazebrouck is conducted by car or by bike, although there are plenty of opportunities to stop and walk.

Using the guide and advice to visitors

Fortunately, the area covered by the guide is dotted with cafés and other refreshment, all of which offer plenty of encouragement to stop and relax. However, this is northern France so be prepared, as the weather can demand a more prudent use of waterproof clothing and walking boots when venturing off the beaten track.

Maps

The tours described in this book are best supported by the IGN Série Bleu 1:25000 maps, which can be purchased at most good tourist offices and online from www.mapsworldwide.com. Cassel is covered by IGN 2303E and 2403O and Hazebrouck by IGN 2404O and 2304E. However, bear in mind that satellite navigation can be a very useful supplement in supporting general route finding, particularly when trying to locate obscure CWGC cemeteries and navigating the streets of Hazebrouck. The Michelin Travel Partner Map can also be downloaded free onto your iPad. In addition, the author would highly recommend using Google Earth or *Geoportail*, the French equivalent, for preparatory work prior to visiting the area.

Travel and where to stay

By far the quickest passage across the Channel is via the Tunnel at Folkstone, the thirty six minutes travelling time comparing favourably with the longer ferry journey from Dover to Calais or Dunkerque. Travelling times vary according to traffic but as a rough guide the journey from Calais to Cassel takes about an hour using the A16 and D916, while Dunkerque to Cassel is some thirty-eight minutes using the D916. Whether your choice of route is over or under the Channel, early booking well in advance is always recommended if advantage is to be taken of the cheaper fares.

If you are intending to base yourself in Cassel the author can recommend both the four-star **Hotel Châtellerie De Schoebeque,** which is situated on the Rue du Maréchal Foch - offering excellent accommodation with the addition of an outdoor swimming pool and spa - and the two-star **Hotel Restaurant de Foch**, which can be found in the Grand Place. Hazebrouck is much less picturesque and the author has no experience of staying in the town; however the three-star **Hotel de Lys** on the Avenue de St-Omer is said to be of reasonable quality. Although a little further afield, the author has personal experience of the three-star **Hotel Belvedere** at Westouter ,which is a short thirty-minute journey across the border into Belgium and benefits from a spacious hotel car park and breakfast, which is included in the daily tariff.

As always, there is a plethora of bed and breakfast and self catering accommodation available on the internet, of these the **Gite et Chambres d'Hôtes du Mont Balenberg** (*gitesetchambresdhotesdumontbalenberg.fr*) situated on the Chemin du Moulin near Noordpeene comes highly recommended; but, again, the author cannot stress enough the importance of early booking.

Campers may appreciate **Camping de Cassel** at Zuytpeene, which has wifi and a number of mobile homes to rent, and **Camping la Chaumiere,** which is a little further west at Buysscheure, but boasts a swimming pool and a restaurant with free wifi. Larger, and very close to the Belgian border, is **Camping du Mont Noir** at Saint-Jans-Cappel, which has a pool and mobile homes to rent, along with plenty of activities for children and free wifi. The campsite is about half an hour from Cassel and is open all year. Further information on all aspects of accommodation can be obtained from the Tourist Office at Cassel, which can be found in the Grand Place and the Hazebrouck Tourist Office in Place du Général de Gaulle.

Driving abroad is not the expedition it was years ago and most battlefield visitors these days may well have already made the journey several times. However, if this is the first time you have ventured on French and Belgian roads there are one or two common sense rules to take into consideration. Ensure your vehicle is properly insured and covered by suitable breakdown insurance; if in doubt contact your insurer, who will advise you. There are also a number of compulsory items to be carried by motorists that are required by French law. These include your driving licence and vehicle registration documents, a warning triangle, a *Conformité Européenne* (CE) approved fluorescent safety vest for each person travelling in the car, headlamp beam convertors and the visible display of a GB plate. Whereas some modern cars have built in headlamp convertors and many have a GB plate incorporated into the rear number plate, French law also requires the vehicle to be equipped with a first aid kit and a breath test kit. If you fail to have these available there are some hefty on the spot fines for these motoring offences if caught driving without them. Most, if not all, of these items can be purchased at the various outlets at the Tunnel and the channel port at Dover and on board the ferries themselves.

Driving on the 'wrong side of the road' can pose some challenges. Here are three tips that the author has always found useful:

1. When driving on single carriageway roads try to stop at petrol stations on the right hand side of the road. It is much more natural then to continue driving on the right hand side of the road after you leave. Leaving a garage or supermarket is often the time when you find yourself naturally turning onto the wrong side of the road.

2. Take your time! Don't rush! If you rush your instinct may take over and your instinct is geared to driving on the left.

3. Pay particular care on roundabouts. A lot of drivers do not and rarely appear to use indicators. Navigators remember to look at the signs anti-clockwise and drivers remember that the danger is coming from the left.

On a more personal note it is always advisable to ensure that your E111 Card is valid in addition to any personal accident insurance you may have; and have a supply of any medication that you may be taking at the time.

Visiting Commonwealth War Graves Commission Cemeteries

The cemeteries visited in this guide are all located in churchyards or in communal cemeteries such as **Hazebrouck Communal Cemetery** and, of these, almost all share their ground with casualties from the final months of the 1914-1918 conflict. The visitor will also come across the graves of aircrew that were shot

down over the course of the war and those men who died during the advance in 1944 after the D-Day landings.

The concept of the Imperial War Graves Commission (IWGC) was created by Major Fabian Ware, the volunteer leader of a Red Cross mobile unit that saw service on the Western Front for most of the period of the First World War. Concern for the identification and burial of the dead led him to begin lobbying for an organization devoted to burial and maintenance of those who had been killed or died in the service of their country. This led to the Prince of Wales becoming the president of the IWGC in May 1917, with Ware as his vice president. Forty-three years later the IWGC became the Commonwealth War

Major Fabian Ware

Commonwealth War Graves Cemetery Sign

Graves Commission (CWGC). The commission was responsible for introducing the standardized headstone, which brought equality in death regardless of rank, race or creed and it is this familiar white headstone that you will see now in CWGC cemeteries all over the world. Where there is a CWGC plot within a communal or churchyard cemetery the familiar green and white sign at the entrance, with the words *Tombes de Guerre du Commonwealth* will indicate their presence. The tall Cross of Sacrifice with the bronze Crusader's sword can be found in the larger cemeteries and a visitor's book and register of casualties is usually kept in the bronze box by the entrance. This may be absent from cemeteries and the register is usually kept in the local Mairie or lodged with the cemetery guardian. Cemetery details can be found at the end of the appropriate tour.

Car Tour 1

Cassel area and Hondegem

Start: The Grand Place in Cassel

Finish: The Grand Place in Cassel

Distance: Twenty-one miles

General Description: This circular tour visits six of the localized actions that were an integral part of the defence of Cassel and provides opportunities to visit four CWGC plots where casualties from those actions are buried. We also visit two impressive blockhouses, one of which is occasionally open to the public.

Route Description: Leave Cassel via the Dunkerkque Gate - Porte de Dunkerque - ❶ onto the D218. The gate can be found near the town war memorial, situated near the Collégiale Notre-Dame de la Crypte at the eastern end of the Grand Place. The area around the Dunkerque Gate contains two significant memorials located below the town war memorial and although these are visited during Walk

The Dunkerque Gate at Cassel

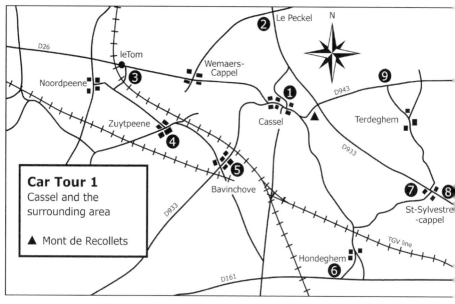

1, they are difficult to ignore! There are two excellent cafes on either side of the gate and one of these would be a good venue from which to begin your tour.

Follow the road through the gate downhill to the junction with the D916 and turn left towards Hardifort. After passing through La Trompe, keep on the D916 until you reach the next crossroads. Turn left here ❷ onto the D338 and then first right along the Chemin de la Wissche to find the Le Peckel blockhouse on your right.

The blockhouse, which was defended by Second Lieutenant Cresswell and 8 Platoon, is now approached via the recently completed access road. Originally used by the farmer to store his potatoes, the bunker has been renovated by Dominique Faivre and members of the Association of Military Historical and

The blockhouse at le Peckel

Archaeological Research (ARHAM) and was officially opened as a memorial on 25 May 2013. The blockhouse is open only on request from the mayor of Hardifort or from ARHAM, which can be contacted at *arham@wanadoo.fr*

From the blockhouse return to the D338 and turn right towards Wemaers-Cappel. As you reach the crossroads in the village the church will be on your left. Turn right along the gently rising D26 to reach the tiny hamlet of le Tom.

Precisely where Second Lieutenant Lanyon positioned his 18-pounder on 26 May is not mentioned in the war diary but there are only two farms and his gun was close to one of them. Local information, however, does suggest the first farm on the left was the only one in existence in May 1940. Parking is difficult, but after turning down the narrow Chemin de Tom, the copse at l'Hey can be seen two miles to the south-west of le Tom, and it was from the flat ground to your left, or close to, that Lanyon's gun shelled the copse when German tanks were spotted amongst the trees. At 1.00pm Sergeant Kibble's carriers arrived and Lanyon's gun supported the recovery of the anti-tank gun, which had been lost earlier at l'Hey by Kibble's patrol.

Zuytpeene is best approached using the Chemin du Tom, which you will find on the right ❸ immediately before the farm. This minor road will take you under the railway line to Nordpeene. Turn left at the junction with the D138 and after

Looking south west down Chemin de Tom. The copse at l'Hey can be seen in the distance, on the right of the photograph

The village of Zuytpeene has changed very little since May 1940.

200 yards you will cross the Lyncke Becque; take care here as it is easy to miss. Immediately after the bridge, the tall memorial to the 1677 Battle of Cassel can be seen on the right, together with an information board. From the memorial follow the road into the village of Zuytpeene ❹ and turn left by the church to follow the D138. With the church now on your right, find a place to park near the village war memorial, which you should be able to see on the right.

The CWGC gravestones are not in the churchyard itself but located behind the village war memorial and accessed through a small metal gate. Zuytpeene is where A Company of the 2/Gloucesters, under Major Bill Percy-Hardman, were sent at 3.45pm on 27 May to stall the German advance.

After leaving the CWGC cemetery, a short walk towards the railway line along Voi Communale la Place will bring you to the building that was, in May 1940, the A Company HQ where Major Percy-Hardman established his command post.

Private Sam Tickner says in his account that A Company HQ was just inside the village after passing under the railway line from Cassel. This certainly places the building along Voi Communale la Place, the exact location of which can be narrowed down to two possibilities. The first is Number 116, which has

114

two barns to the rear, this fits Tickner's description of the building where he describes moving his vehicle off the road. However, pre-war aerial photographs of the village do show another building, which was on the site of the present day allotment to the right of No.116, which could also have been Percy-Hardman's HQ. Local information indicates both buildings were severely damaged by fire in May 1940 and one was not rebuilt. Precisely which one housed Percy-Hardman's HQ remains clouded by time, but the author's preference leans towards No.116.

The remaining section posts from 7 and 9 Platoons were deployed around the church. The Gloucesters had a great deal of difficulty in convincing the local inhabitants to leave as the Germans were close by and would be arriving soon, a situation that prompted Gilmore to visit the village at 8.30am to see the situation for himself. Finding that many of the villagers were still in situ, he noted that the A Company platoons were having difficulty in positioning tank-proof locations and many of the company posts were in the open, a concern he must have voiced to Percy-Hardman before he left to return to Cassel. The German attack began at 10.00am on 27 May.

Private Vaughan says that 9 Platoon was in the village near Company HQ and he and Private Price were sent by PSM Oxtoby to Cassel to ask for reinforcements passing by A Company HQ, which, Vaughan says, had been demolished by shellfire and was on fire. This may have been roughly at the same time that Privates Tickner and Bennet were sent to Cassel to report to Gilmore, having left Zuytpeene at about 3.30pm. When they left the village the company was surrounded and there had been many casualties. Both thought that Major Percy Hardman was dead.

Return to your vehicle and continue along the Voi Communale la Place (D138) towards Bavinchove ❺ keeping the railway line on your left. On entering the village along Rue de Fleurs, the church will be on your right. Park here and walk through the gate at the rear of the church to find the CWGC plot immediately to your left. On returning to your vehicle continue straight ahead and take the next left, turning into Rue de Cassel. Just before the level crossing turn right into Rue de la Gare and park at the junction with the D933. Walk up to the level crossing.

The village was defended by Captain Charles Clutsom and D Company of the 4/Ox and Bucks. Much less is known about this action but from the small number of accounts that have survived the ravages of time it would appear the 4/Ox and Bucks blocked the railway line with two locomotives and various rolling stock and defended the village to the north of the railway line. Second Lieutenant Wallis confirms that D Company were attacked by motorcycle troops, troops in lorries and about six tanks. His single 25mm anti-tank gun was in position on the railway line firing across the road and put four German AFVs out of action. Wallis does not say exactly where the gun was, but it was very probably east of the level crossing where you are now standing, positioned at the point where the line is on a slight embankment. Once the Germans began outflanking them and

The level crossing at Bavinchove. German engineers are in the process of moving the stationary train while a Panzer IV is positioned on the right.

the crew came under German machine gun fire, the gun was abandoned, but not before Private Blake was killed.

Return to your vehicle and take the left hand turning along D138 under the TGV railway line and continue for 1.7 miles to meet the old Roman road. Turn right here and at the next crossroads turn left along the D161. Continue until you reach a minor crossroads, where a left turn – Kalverstraet - leads into Hondeghem ❻ along a minor road. If you are intending to pause here, it is better to pull off the road before you turn left into Kalverstraet.

The road you have just travelled down is the route taken by *Hauptmann* Löwe

The same scene today

The turning from the D161 – Kalverstraet – which leads to the center of Hondeghem

and continues into Caëstre, where his column came up against 133 Brigade. This is the approximate position of the first road block and the J Subsection gun was positioned on the road some fifty yards further down the road ahead of you. In the farm buildings, which you can see behind you and north of the road, a small garrison had been deployed to bring fire onto any approaching vehicles. A similar arrangement surrounded the I Subsection gun, which was in position half a mile further east on the D161 where there is now a roundabout.

It is likely that *Leutnant* Kelletat and his men approached the village along Kalverstraet which at least offered some cover from the by now rapid fire emanating from the defending garrison. The street layout of the village remains the same as it was in May 1940, the only difference being that the railway line

The Mairie at Hondeghem

The moated house on Kalverstraet where a probable ambush of German forces took place

and its station is no longer in existence. Continue into Hondeghem, pausing at the moated house on the left, where the two German vehicles were ditched. These vehicles were almost certainly carrying infantry reinforcements and were probably ambushed on the bend in the road.

Turn left at the junction and then bear left at the fork in the road and stop at the junction with the D53. Straight ahead is Rue de St-Marie-Cappel and, to your right, the road leads to the church. This junction is the likely position of the L Subsection gun after it was moved from its initial position at the crossroads behind the *Mairie*. Continue straight ahead on Rue de St-Marie-Cappel for seventy yards to reach the next staggered crossroads. This was the first position of the L Subsection gun, which was defending the narrow road approaching the village from the west. The crew would have moved the gun to its second position after it became apparent the enemy attack was being directed from the direction of the D161.

Turn right at the staggered crossroads along the narrow Rue de la Mairie and park by the church. The church tower, which was destroyed by the Germans, is the location from which the artillery barrage from Mont des Récollets was directed and brought *Leutnant* Kelletat's men to a halt. On the corner of the Rue de la Mairie is the school building and further along the road, opposite the churchyard, is where Battery HQ was established in the *Mairie* building. We are now going to visit the churchyard cemetery, so, keeping the church on your right, and a row of private houses on your left, walk down the road to access the gate into the churchyard; the British graves are on the right as you enter.

After leaving the churchyard, turn right and walk down to where Rue de la K. Hondeghem Battery joins the main square. This is where the K Subsection gun was positioned, pointing straight down the road towards the D161. To your right is a row of houses bordering the main square and the cookhouse was in a building along here. It is more than likely that the L Subsection gun destroyed the building, but whether the building was situated where Number 207 stands

The church tower at Hondeghem was used as an observation post by 5/RHA

today is anyone's guess. However, photographs of the village taken from the air in 1938 indicate the row of buildings that bordered the road was continuous and there was no gap where Number 207 stands today, making that location a strong contender for the position of the former cookhouse.

From Hondeghem head north out of the village along the D53, which is the route Rawdon Hoare and his men took when they left the church square. Take the first turning on the right after crossing over the TGV railway line, this minor road will take you to St-Sylvestre-Cappel. ❼ As you enter the village the church is on your left. Turn left into the Place de l' Église and park.

It was when the K Battery men arrived at St-Sylvestre-Cappel that the main road was found to be blocked and orders were given to take up positions around the church. A fierce fire-fight broke out as German troops appeared on all sides. Captain Teacher was left with little choice but to dislodge the Germans in the churchyard with a bayonet charge, and two parties of British troops made their way around each side of the churchyard. In the resulting confusion of battle the Germans withdrew, in what was described as 'a panic stricken rout', with some throwing away their weapons. But the situation was still desperate and

119

the British were still surrounded. Both guns were now brought into action to disperse German strong-points that had been established in the surrounding houses. Soon after this, the K Subsection gun and its Quad was put out of action by two direct hits, and finally, after abandoning the L Subsection gun, the party had little choice but to run the gauntlet of fire and make their escape.

Leave your car at Place de l' Église and walk along to the junction with the D916. Turn right here and walk up the road for 130 yards to where you can see a signpost ❽ for the *Cimetière*. Cross the road – take care here as it can very busy – and enter the cemetery. The CWGC plot is immediately on your left. After leaving the cemetery turn left and continue up the road for another 200 yards until you see the entrance to a green lane on the right. This leads directly to an enormous WW2 blockhouse that is almost invisible from the road. The entrance is locked but it is possible to climb the narrow staircase to the former cupola. After your visit to the bunker, return down hill to the church and your vehicle.

Keeping the church on your right, continue around the churchyard to reach the junction with the D916. Imagine for a moment the looks on the faces of the artillerymen when they glanced left and right to see a German tank blocking the road in both directions. Their only route now lay along Rue de Terdeghem, a narrow road which you can see almost opposite you.

Cross the road with care and after following the first bend in the road, park by the metal gates, which you can see ahead of you. Now turn round to face the direction you have just taken. In May 1940 a German machine gun was positioned on the first bend, which forced the escaping artillerymen to drive through the bends in the road bends at speed. The metal gates are where the driver of the second vehicle completely missed the next turning and drove through the hedge into the field beyond. Today the field contains a post-war housing development,

The blockhouse on the D916 at St-Sylvestre-Cappel

The gate marks the point at which a 5/RHA vehicle crashed through the hedge during their escape from St-Sylvestre-Cappel

but fortunately, seventy-six years previously, the ground was dry and the driver rejoined the road further on by crashing through some railings about 150 yards before the crossroads.

As the road turns sharp right again, you will pass a row of private houses on the left; it was along here that the first vehicle took the second bend too fast and ditched by the side of the road, the occupants successfully clambering into the third vehicle and escaping. After a mile or so the surviving men of 5/RHA met an incredulous C Squadron of the East Riding Yeomanry, who had just mined the road along which they had passed.

Continue through the bends and go straight ahead at the crossroads, after which you will reach Terdeghem, where signposts for Cassel will direct you to the D948. At the junction with the D948 ❾ turn left, and pass the Mont des Récollets on your left, from where the Grand Place in Cassel is just a few minutes away.

Zuytpeene Churchyard Cemetery

The crew of a Lancaster III was shot down by a night fighter on the night of 23/24 June 1944 after returning from bombing the V1 Site at Coubronne. Of those that remained with the aircraft, all were killed with the exception of the bomb aimer, **Sergeant Price**, who was taken prisoner. The Pilot, **P/O Dennis Langford**, managed to use his parachute and it is thought he was murdered by

The CWGC plot at Zuytpeene

German forces. His name is commemorated on the Runnymede Memorial. The three men from the 2/Gloucesters were found in the church tower much later in 1940/41. They had been killed during A Company's defence of the village and lay undiscovered until local villagers noticed a strange odour coming from the tower! Hence the dates of their deaths are recorded imprecisely on the CWGC database.

Bavinchove Churchyard Cemetery

There is one unidentified casualty buried here. Apart from **Pte George Blake**, who was killed serving with 145 Brigade Anti-Tank Company, the remaining five identified 4/Ox and Bucks men are probably from the D Company action on 27 May. **Sergeant Christopher Lloyd** was serving with the 1/Fife and Forfar Yeomanry and was killed after taking a wrong turning en-route to Hondeghem running into units of the 6th Panzer Division.

Hondeghem Churchyard Cemetery

There are seven casualties from 1918 buried here. **Lieutenant Arthur Addey-Jibb** was 29-years-old when he died of wounds after shellfire hit his Advanced

Hondeghem Churchyard Cemetery

Dressing Station. Buried with him are **Privates John Brook** and **John Eccles** and **Sergeant George Mobray**, all from 95 Field Ambulance and killed in the same action. New Zealander **Captain Roland Hill** of the 2/Otago Regiment had been decorated with the MC and mentioned in despatches when he and **Second Lieutenant Duncan Mclean** were shot on 3 March by **Private Avon Roderique**. After being told by Hill that he was probably returning to the front line, Roderique shot both officers and then turned his gun on himself. McLean had been awarded the MM in 1917 shortly before he was commissioned and went on to be mentioned twice in despatches. Roderique is buried at Hazebrouck Communal Cemetery. **BSM James Murphy** was another decorated soldier who had been awarded the DCM and mentioned in despatches before his death in May whilst serving with C Battery, 148 Artillery Brigade. The two 1940 casualties are undoubtedly from the Hondeghem encounter. **Bombardier John Turner** was serving with 2/Searchlight Regiment and **Gunner Albert Adaway** was an artilleryman with 5/RHA. He is also commemorated in St Margaret's Church, South Wonston, near Winchester.

St-Sylvestre-Cappel New Cemetery

Of the nineteen casualties from May 1940, four remain unidentified, their names being inscribed on a single headstone. The two men from the East Riding

123

St-Sylvestre-Cappel Communal Cemetery

Yeomanry were casualties from the B Squadron clash on 26 May with units of the 6th Panzer Division near St-Sylvestre-Cappel. **TSM Thomas Wyatt Arbon** was leading 4 Troop when a direct hit on his carrier killed him and badly wounded 21-year-old **Trooper Herbert Ostler**. Ostler died of wounds on 27 May, the day before his older brother, Trooper William Ostler, was killed serving with the same regiment. The eleven identified graves of men from 5/RHA are probably all casualties from the fighting in St-Sylvestre-Cappel; of these, the CWGC database lists three men whose date of death cannot be verified exactly, but the author is of the opinion that these men were victims of the fighting on 27 May.

Walk 1

Cassel Town East

Start: Place du Général Vandamme

Finish: Place du Général Vandamme

Distance: Three miles

General Description: This circular walk begins in the small square that was, until 1980, named Place du Général Plumer. We visit the company positions occupied by the 2/Gloucesters before visiting the communal cemetery and part of the perimeter where the 4/Ox and Bucks were deployed. The tour also takes in the views from the summit and the principle buildings in the Grand Place. There is no map for this walk as a good street plan of Cassel can be obtained from the Tourist Office which you will find next door to the Departmental Museum of Flanders in the Grand Place.

Route Description: Major Gilmore established the 2/Gloucesters' HQ in the cellars of the **Credit du Nord Bank**, which you can see on the southern side

Major Gilmore established his headquarters in the cellars of the Credit du Nord Bank

of the square. Outside, along the edge of the pavement, a parapet of sandbags was erected to prevent blast entering the cellars. The Battalion Aid Post (RAP), under the command of Lieutenant Ian Spencer RAMC, was located nearby. The buildings on either side were also occupied by the Gloucesters and the area is referred to in Eric Jones' diary as the 'Keep'. It was here that Major Percy-Hardman and A Company was positioned prior to being relocated to **Zuytpeene**. Brigade HQ was also based here for a while and presumably occupied one of the buildings in the same row as the bank. In the latter stages of the defence, 140/Field Regiment positioned two of its guns in the square.

General Sir Herbert Plumer had his Second Army headquarters in the Castel Yvonne during his stay in Cassel in 1916

The former tram depot is now a community centre

To the left of the bank you can see **Castel Yvonne** in the Rue St Nicholas, where General Plumer resided during the First World War. If you turn and face east you will be able to see the former tram depot, from where passengers were transported to Bavinchove railway station. Today the service has been replaced by a scheduled bus service and the depot has been converted into a community centre. To the left of the community centre the tall radio mast of the Gendamerie can be seen on Rue de Bergues, which is where the 4/Ox and Bucks had their battalion HQ along with the East Riding Yeomanry. It was in the basement of that building that Major Joe Thorne of the Ox and Bucks was killed by shellfire.

Now walk south to the junction with Rue Bollaert le Gavrain and turn right. The narrow entrance to **Rue des Ramparts** is by House Number 5 and at the time of writing is marked by a wooden way marked signpost. Walk down the passageway and where the track breaks out into the open countryside and stop. This was the C Company area, commanded by Captain Esmond Harcourt Lynn-Allen, whose MC was gazetted in 1945. Lynn-Allen did not keep an account of C Company's fight at Cassel but when Major Gilmore and Eric Jones toured the Gloucesters' company defences on Monday evening, they noted there had been considerable number of casualties and an 'appreciable number of enemy tanks lying derelict in open country, particularly opposite C Company', which Gilmore attributed to good shooting with the Boys anti-tank rifle. Whilst in captivity Lynn-Allen wrote *Rough Shoot: Some thoughts for the Owner-Keeper,* a book of sporting reminiscences written with Captain John Elphinstone - later the 17th Lord Elphinstone.

Across to your right is where 13 Platoon (Lieutenant J N Rice) was positioned – their area ran for a short distance downhill to two wooded copses. On the

The Porte d'Aire pictured before the war

left of the path was 15 Platoon, which was positioned in and amongst the houses and gardens bordering the Grand Place. Continue and cross over the Rue de l'Infermerie, walking on to the next junction of tracks. This is where 14 Platoon were positioned, with their section posts running downhill almost alongside Rue d'Aire. Turn right here and walk down the Rue d'Aire – the 14 Platoon posts being on your right; if you look behind you, the Porte d'Aire can be seen guarding the entrance to the Grand Place. Take the first left - Chemin du Tilleaul - which will take you back uphill. After the left hand bend the Rue des Ramparts appears again on your right, continue along here until you reach the ornamental bridge that crosses the pathway above you.

You are now in the area defended by A Company of the Ox and Bucks. It is from somewhere along here that Lieutenant Duncan watched the encirclement of Bavinchove by German motorised units while standing with Captain Pat Rathcreedan. Turn left here, passing under four brick archways, to reach the junction with Rue Maréchal Foch. Turn right and in eighty yards stop outside

During his stay at Cassel Ferdinand Foch lived in the Hôtel de Schoebeque on the Rue du Maréchal Foch, which, at the time, was a private house

LE MARECHAL FOCH
ALORS GÉNÉRAL COMMANDANT EN CHEF
LES ARMÉES DU NORD
RÉSIDA DANS CETTE MAISON
DU 24 OCTOBRE 1914 AU 9 MAI 1915
IL Y REVINT ENSUITE
À DIVERSES REPRISES NOTAMMENT
PENDANT LA BATAILLE DU
MONT KEMMEL
IL Y RECUT DE NOMBREUSES PERSONNALITÉS
S.M. ALBERT I⁽ᴱᴿ⁾ ROI DES BELGES
S.A.R. LE PRINCE DE GALLES
LE MARÉCHAL JOFFRE
LE GÉNÉRAL DE MAUD' HUY
LE GÉNÉRAL MAISTRE

S.M. GEORGES V
ROI DE GRANDE BRETAGNE ET D'IRLANDE
EMPEREUR DES INDES
ACCOMPAGNÉ DE S.A.R. LE PRINCE DE GALLES
RÉSIDA DANS CETTE MAISON
DU 12 AU 16 AOÛT 1916 ET DU 3 AU 7 JUILLET 1917

LE MARÉCHAL DOUGLAS HAIG
COMMANDANT EN CHEF L' ARMÉE ANGLAISE
Y SÉJOURNA
EN 1916 DU 26 AU 30 AVRIL-DU 9 AU 12 MAI -
- DU 18 AU 23 DÉCEMBRE
EN 1917 27 FÉVRIER-DU 21 AU 26 MAI-15 AOÛT -
2 OCTOBRE-4 OCTOBRE-DU 8 AU 15 OCTOBRE
EN 1919 DU 21 AU 27 MARS.

The memorial plaque above the entrance to the Hôtel de Schoebeque

the **Hôtel Schoebeque**, which you will see marked by the flags ahead of you. This is where Foch lived while he was resident in Cassel and received guests such as King George V and the Prince of Wales. To the left of the entrance gate a memorial plaque commemorates the building's connection with Foch and Field Marshal Haig, who also used the building as his residence when in the area.

Continue straight ahead, following the road round to the left to reach **Dead Horse Corner** and the communal cemetery. A new memorial has recently been placed near the road, close to the cemetery, commemorating the point where French forces halted the German advance in 1914. Enter the cemetery by the gate leading to the small domed chapel. Amongst the myriad of sepulchres and tombstones you will find the grave of Général Dominique-Joseph Vandamme, which is marked by a small column, and the grave of *Capitane* Archille Samyn, the owner of the Villa de Moulins, who was killed at Dunkerque in May

The grave of Général Dominique-Joseph Vandamme, is marked by a small column

1940. Walk on through the communal cemetery until you reach the CWGC plot, from where good views of the nearby Mont de Récollets can be had.

After leaving the cemetery via the second gate near the CWGC plot, walk down the road for a few metres to the Chemin de Cornette. The ground to your left drops away towards numerous post-war houses; but in May 1940 there were only a small number of private houses, and it was in these that 145 Brigade and the 2/Gloucesters first established their headquarters. Further down, and close to the D916 opposite the **Château Masson**, is where 140/Field Regiment positioned their guns. This area came under a heavy attack on 27 May and German forces almost succeeded in penetrating the Cassel perimeter, prompting the various battalion and regimental headquarters to retire to the comparative safety of Cassel itself. The attack was finally brought to a halt by Lieutenant Charlie Clerke Brown's carriers and a party of the Ox and Bucks, led by CSM Cecil Bailey from A Company, who pushed the Germans out of the Château Masson grounds.

Retrace your steps and walk uphill to find the narrow Chemin de Chapitre. Continue past the shrine, bearing left at the metal gates, to reach the steps leading up to Rue Notre Dame. This is the area defended by C Company of the Ox and Bucks. As you climb the steps you will see the disused 17th century Jesuit church high up on your left, another view can be had once you reach Rue Notre Dame. At the top of the steps turn right and stop outside house Number 5. It is thought that this house was the Ox and Bucks C Company HQ and was from where

Rue Notre Dame where it is thought the Ox and Bucks C Company HQ was situated

The Gloucesters' memorial

DEDICATED TO THE MEMORY OF THE OFFICERS AND MEN OF THE
4ᵗʰ (TA) BATTALION, THE OXFORDSHIRE & BUCKINGHAMSHIRE LIGHT INFANTRY
WHO FOUGHT AND DIED FROM WATERLOO TO CASSEL COVERING THE
EVACUATION OF THE BRITISH AND FRENCH FORCES AT DUNKIRK
✠ 14TH-29TH MAY 1940 ✠

The 4/Ox and Bucks memorial

In proud memory of Brigadier The Honourable NFSomerset CBE, D.S.O., M.C., and the 228 officers and men of The 2ⁿᵈ & 5ᵗʰ Battalions, The Gloucestershire Regiment, who fought and died from Waterloo to Cassel & Ledringhem covering the evacuation of the British and French forces at Dunkirk 14 - 29 May 1940.

the Rev David Wild watched C and D Companies of the 9/Notts and Derby Regiment (Sherwood Foresters) debussing in the Grand Place. Hit by marauding Stukas, four casualties from that attack can be found in the communal cemetery.

Now walk down to the town war memorial and on the wall to the right of the **Dunkerque Gate** are two plaques commemorating the actions of the Gloucesters and Ox and Bucks in the town during May 1940. It is also possible that one of the

The bronze medallion inside the Collégiale Notre-Dame de la Crypte which was erected in Foch's honour and unveiled by his widow in 1933

The Grand Place looking east towards the Collégiale Notre-Dame de la Crypte

two cafés that stand either side of the Dunkerque Gate housed the headquarters of F Troop, 140/Field Regiment. The position of Regimental headquarters was thought to be further along Rue de Bergues.

You are now in the Grand Place, with the towering presence of the **Collégiale Notre-Dame de la Crypte** dominating its eastern end. The church, which is usually open, is worth a visit and is where the plaque commemorating Foch's son and son-in-law can be found. There is also a large bronze medallion placed in his

The Hôtel du Sauvage pictured during the uneasy peace between the wars

honour by his widow and unveiled in 1933. Walk on into the square, where there are numerous opportunities to take a break for refreshment. Straight ahead of you is the neo Flemish facade of the **Hôtel du Sauvage**, where the famous meeting took place on 27 May; it is no longer a hotel but would still be instantly recognizable to those officers and men who visited Cassel during the First World War. The restaurant has since been extended and offers wonderful views over the Flanders plain. Keeping to the left hand side of the Grand Place you will soon arrive at Number 16, the **Tourist Office**, with the **Departmental Museum of Flanders** next door. This is the former **Hôtel de la Noble Cour** – also known as

The building used by 145/Field Ambulance

Landshuys - where Foch had his headquarters from 23 October 1914 to 9 May 1915. His Chief of Staff throughout the war was **Maxime Wegand**, who had an office in the same building. It was Wegand that surrendered France to the Germans in 1940. On the corner of Rue d'Aire is the building that was occupied

by 143/Field Ambulance and where **Major Lawson** established his field hospital. At the time of writing the building was unoccupied and in a poor state of repair. The museum, which covers local history and has memorials from the Crimean and Franco-Prussian wars, is well worth a visit. As you leave the museum a glance down Rue d'Aire will reveal the **Porte d'Aire**, made famous by the William Orpen painting.

The rebuilt *Mairie*, where Lieutenant Colonel Thompson visited Brigadier Somerset's headquarters in the cellars

The Casino before it was demolished

Now cross over to the far side of the Grand Place to the rebuilt *Mairie*, where Lieutenant Colonel Thompson visited Brigadier Somerset's headquarters in the cellars. The original building dated back to 1643 and was completely destroyed by fire in May 1940. Walk on past the *Mairie* and take the right turning uphill into Place Queux de Saint Hilaire. Ahead you will see a set of ornamental concrete steps, which lead to the public park above, while immediately to the right of the steps is the narrow cobbled **Rue Alexis Bafcop**. At the top of the steps

the foundations of the former Casino building are on the right, while straight ahead of you is the monument to the three battles of Cassel. Further on, past the private house, the imposing statue of **Maréchal Foch** on horseback stands in front of a single windmill, which was brought here from Arnèke. The windmill symbolises the twenty-two mills which once graced this highpoint at the beginning of the 20th century. The statue of Foch was sculpted by Georges Malissard and unveiled by President Poincaré in 1928. Foch died a few months later, in March 1929. Before you leave, take advantage of the views to the north and south, which are exceptionally fine and benefit

The Three Battles Monument

from the addition of orientation tables carved into the edging stones that surround the park. From the park take the narrow cobbled path downhill, which leads directly to the Place du *Général* Vandamme and your vehicle.

Cassel Communal Cemetery Extension

There are now nearly one hundred casualties from the Second World War commemorated in this site. Of these, forty-two were killed between 24 and 29 May 1940. Amongst the dead of the 2/Gloucesters you will find 21-year-old **Second Lieutenant Gerald French** (C.8.), 33-year-old **PSM William Rumble** (A.7.), from Frilsham in Berkshire, and 27-year-old **Second Lieutenant George Weightma**n (C.6.), who was a graduate of Durham University and working as a teacher in 1939. Two names of Gloucestershire soldiers, 25-year-old **Corporal Alsace Larraine Brisland** (C.7.) and **Private James Neale** (A.6.) both appear on the same Berkeley War Memorial in the church of St Mary the Virgin, Berkeley, Gloucestershire. **Captain Edward 'Roger' Dixie** (B.22.) commanded 145 Brigade Anti-Tank Company and Shanghai born 40-year-old **Major Joseph 'Joe' Thorne** (B.21.) was second in command of the Ox and Bucks. Thorne hailed from Southam in Warwickshire and was married to Marjorie Catherine Thorne. His two older brothers were killed

Cassel Communal Cemetery Extension. Mont de Récollets can be seen in the background

serving with the East Surreys in the First World War – Thorne was a mere 15 years old at the time. Joe Thorne is in the same row as two of the four of 9/Notts and Derby soldiers killed in the *Luftwaffe* attack witnessed by David Wild.

Amongst the British dead are twelve Czech Army graves from the 1/Czech Armoured Brigade action in 1945. Their headstones are of a different shape to the CWGC standard pattern and represent some of the last allied troops to be killed in this vicinity during the Second World War. For those who are struggling with the different rank descriptions the following may be of some help:

Vojin	–	Private
Svobodnik	–	Private 1st Class
Četar	–	Sergeant
Rotmistr	–	Sergeant 1st Class
Poruĉik	–	Second Lieutenant

The single casualty from the RAAF was shot down by a Me109 from JG26 on 9 May 1942. 24-year-old **Sergeant William James Smith** (E.6.) was one of two pilots flying Spitfire Vbs that were lost from 457 Squadron during the 'Circus 160' raid on the enemy coast.

Walk 2

Cassel and the Western Approaches

Start: Rue de Watten

Finish: Chemin Particulier

Distance: Two miles

General Description: This is a circular walk that begins ❶ on D11 - Rue de Watten - where the D933 – Avenue Achille Samyn – forks left to continue downhill towards the Catholic College of Saint-Marie. The memorial to Dominique-Joseph Vandamme is at the junction of these two roads. We follow the B Company position's on the D11 before moving downhill past Weightman's farm to the junction with the D52 at la Croix Rouge. Here we leave the road and walk around the western edge of the former château grounds to arrive back on the Rue de Watten. In May 1940 the château was called Villa de Moulins and was surrounded by magnificent park that contained a number of windmills; it was in these grounds that D Company established themselves. The château building was destroyed in May 1940 and the present house was not finally erected until some years after the war. All that remains today of the former Villa de Moulins is the gatehouse on Avenue Achille Samyn and a section of perimeter wall facing the D933.

Captain Bill Wilson most probably had his B Company HQ at Number 36

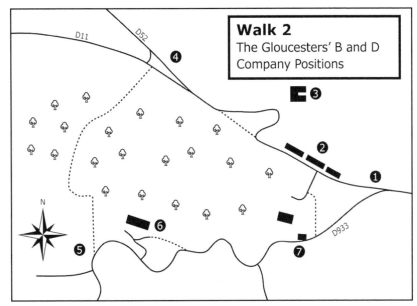

Route Description: Our walk begins at the fork in the road where the houses on the northern side of the road – your right - were defended and occupied by **PSM Morgan** and the men of **11 Platoon**. At one point in the battle there were two anti-tank guns positioned 'wheel to wheel' here. Captain Wilson's Company HQ was probably at house Number 36, as local information suggests this building ❷ was badly damaged by shell fire and Wilson himself reported the house received

Second Lieutenant Julian Fane and the men of 11 Platoon occupied the last houses on the right

Second Lieutenant George Weightman and 10 Platoon were in the farm buildings north of Rue de Watten

a direct hit on 27 May. This is also where **Lance Corporal Greenhough** saw the gun from 140/Field Regiment hit by German mortar fire on 29 May and witnessed the death of **Second Lieutenant Gerald French**. PSM Morgan was badly wounded in the same attack. Before you continue along the road, note the narrow Chemin Particulier on the left, almost opposite Number 36; it is along this narrow alleyway that you will return to the Rue de Watten at the end of the tour.

Continue along Rue de Watten to where **Second Lieutenant Fane** and **12 Platoon** occupied the final few houses on Rue de Watten. From the rear of the buildings the fields of fire and observation opportunities over the northern aspects of the approaches to Cassel were first class. Further along, and much lower down the slope, Wilson positioned **Second Lieutenant George Weightman** and **10 Platoon ❸** in the farm, which you should be able to glimpse as you walk downhill. Where the road bends sharply to the right, a path appears on the edge of the wood to the left of a small telephone junction box. Take this steep little pathway which, although paved, can be slippery in wet weather. (The alternative route takes you along the road and through the bends, from where a better view of Weightman's Farm can be had. If you choose this route beware of speeding traffic.) As you descend the pathway, note that 16 Platoon and **Second Lieutenant Charlesworth** from D Company were dug into positions on your left, a view that is now almost entirely obscured by trees and shrubs.

Once you have rejoined the road, continue downhill to the junction with

The fork in the road at La Croix Rouge

the D52. This is the la Croix Rouge junction ❹ where the **Macforce** column was stopped on 24 May by **Lieutenant Colonel Templar** and K Battery from 5/RHA was diverted to Hondeghem. This is also where the forward 2/Gloucester units reported seeing enemy tanks and embussed infantry early on 27 May. Just opposite the road junction a grass path on the left leads down to the edge of the wood which, at the time of writing, is marked by a wooden way-marked

The path which follows the perimeter of the château park

signpost. Take this path and enter the wood along the path, bearing left as it winds its way through the trees. The path, which can be muddy in wet weather, then rises steeply, following a wire fence on your left.

You are now walking along the perimeter of the château park that contained the former Villa de Moulins; the trees and shrubs you can see were not in existence in May 1940, but there were a number of windmills situated on the higher ground. Pass a large metal gate on your left and bear right towards the farm from where the new château building now comes into view across to your left. Glancing right, there are good views over the Flander's plain towards Wormhout and Dunkerque.

At the junction ❺ with the D933 turn left towards the college building you can see ahead of you. The road rises gently uphill and after some 150 yards you pass what looks like a private house on the left. This is the entrance to the **Saint-Marie College** grounds and the narrow vehicle access leads directly up to the college buildings. The buildings ❻ now house a private Catholic college that caters for day and boarding pupils. Looking at the front of the college the original building can be clearly seen on the left, the upper floors of which were damaged during the fighting in May 1940.

It was probably from here that the Germans attempted to establish a post in

The Saint-Marie College. The original building, which was damaged in May 1940, can be seen on the left

The gatehouse to the former Villa de Moulins

the corner of the Villa de Moulins grounds and where the German tanks got into the grounds through **17 Platoon's** positions. It is in this corner of the grounds that **Captain Cholmondeley** and a party of six men from D Company, counter attacked and drove the enemy off without loss to themselves. We will return to this action later.

Continue up the road along the pathway on the right, passing the Chemin de Ryckewaert. As you enter the outskirts of Cassel notice the original walls of the Villa de Moulins on the left, while a hundred yards further ahead is the gatehouse ❼ guarding the entrance drive to the former Villa de Moulins grounds. In May 1940 the Villa was much closer to the road from where the reconstructed modern building stands today. During the brief stay by D Company of the 2/ Gloucesters, the villa was occupied by **18 Platoon** under the command of **PSM Rumble**, while Captain Cholmondeley established his Company HQ in one of the two *pigeonaires* further back in the grounds. Sadly, there is no trace today of the former Villa de Moulins, which was owned by Achille Samyn, but the road you are walking along is named in his memory. The villa was destroyed in 1940 by shellfire and German bombing. Samyn's widow never returned to Cassel, leaving her former home to fall into almost total ruin. The present building was not completed until 1970.

The rebuilt villa is home to Dominique Billiet

Immediately after the gatehouse you will find a block of three garages with a balustrade standing above them; tucked away between the end of the garages and the private house are a set of steps. Take these steps, which lead to a narrow pathway winding its way uphill towards Chemin Particulier. Where the path takes a sharp left turn you can look across to the left into the former château park grounds. The long low building you can see was originally built post-war as a piggery but today serves as an art studio; the wooded mound you can see near the gates was the site of one of two former *pigeonaires,* which were built in the north of the property. The present owner of the property tells us that the *pigeonaire* was in fact one of the former windmills that graced the property. Whether the mound you can see was where Captain Wilson found Cholmondeley 'surrounded by wounded' is difficult to say precisely, but according to local information it is the most likely spot.

Where the path joins Chemin Particulier stop. This is the road along which Captain Wilson ran after being told tanks were in the D Company area. Where the large gate to the château grounds stands is most probably where he found 'about forty troops of D Company and the B[attalio]n Mortar Platoon, collected, standing like lost sheep'; repositioning the men, he then found a very dazed Cholmoneley in the *Pigeonaire,* which may have prompted him to search for

143

The narrow Chemin Particulier

the tank. Running back to B Company on Rue de Watten, he gathered together a small group and a Boys rifle and set off back into the château park. It was while he was stalking the tank that they were fired upon by the Gloucesters' Mortar Platoon. His own account tells us that on his return he climbed to an observation post, in the D Company HQ building, where he saw the tank had been disabled by an anti-tank gun.

Continue down Chemin Particulier to reach Rue de Watten and turn right to find your vehicle.

Car Tour 2

The Hazebrouck Defences

Start: The crossroads at les Cinq Rues on the D642

Finish: Place du Général de Gaulle, Hazebrouck

Distance: Ten miles

General Description: there is no specific map for this tour as the street map supplied by the tourist Information Office in Place du Général de Gaulle provides a very good overview of the town and you may wish to call in here before you begin the tour. However, please bear in mind that Sunday and Monday mornings are when the market uses Place du Général de Gaulle. Our tour begins on the western approach to the town at the les Cinq Rues crossroads and after visiting the likely positions of D Company we move south to the C Company area in and around the Trocadero area of the town. We then move north again to the area around the railway station to visit B Company before returning to Place du Général de Gaulle from where it is a short walk to the Rue de la Sous- Préfécture, where the reconstructed orphanage building and the Instutut St Jacques can be found. It is suggested a visit to the Communal Cemetery takes place after you have completed the tour. The author found satellite navigation to be very useful in navigating around the streets of Hazebrouck.

Place du Général de Gaulle

Route Description: Les Cinq Rues is where the 392/Battery gun under the command of **Sergeant Mordin** engaged the leading units of the 8th Panzer Division on 24 May. If you turn left and follow the road down to the railway crossing you will be at the spot where **Second Lieutenant Sandy Powell**, commanding **17 Platoon**, saw the German reconnaissance patrol on the morning of 27 May, which was fired upon by a 25-pounder from 392/Battery. Retrace your steps to the main road and continue towards Hazebrouck; cross over the next roundabout - **Second Lieutenant Amyas Lee** and the men of **16 Platoon** were astride the road and railway line here. Having passed over another roundabout you will arrive at a third roundabout, where the road takes you left under the railway line. At the next roundabout turn left again into Avenue de la Haute Loge. Slow down here, as on the left you will see a signal box indicating the position of the level crossing, which at the time of writing was closed. This is where **9 Platoon** from A Company were positioned. By continuing past the level crossing along the Grand Chemin de Cassel and following the road as it bears round to the right, you will come to a junction, stop here. The D642 Hazebrouck Ring Road is on your left and, although there is little to see today, **7 Platoon** from A Company, commanded by **Second Lieutenant Michael Sherwell**, was situated in and around a farmhouse that once stood here on the town boundary. The two A Company platoons were deployed as a result of **Captain Saunder's** request for reinforcements and his concern regarding the northern sector of the town. At some point in the morning of 27 May, Sherwell and **7 Platoon** were driven out of their positions and sent to reinforce C Company.

You are now going to retrace your steps to the roundabout on Avenue de la Haute Loge. Turn right to go back under the underpass and then turn almost immediately right again at the next roundabout. You should now be travelling along the Avenue St-Omer, a route that takes you back past the level crossing where **9 Platoon** was positioned. Continue for another 250 yards to the small roundabout and turn left down Rue de Calais. Just after the road bends you will see Petit Rue de Sercus on your right; take care here as the turning is a sharp one. Pause here.

Sadly there is very little to see of the remaining D Company platoon posts. **Second Lieutenant Sandy Powell** and **17 Platoon** is described as being in the Petite Rue de Sercus area and situated some 200 yards further south than **16 Platoon**, who we know were astride the railway and road north of Rue de Calais. Saunders established Company HQ in a farmhouse on the town boundary that disappeared many years ago. However, the positions occupied by **Second Lieutenant Tom Garside** and **18 Platoon** are still in evidence and the farmhouse where he and his platoon were initially positioned by Saunders is our next port of call.

Continue through the bends on Petit Rue de Sercus until the road narrows, keeping the large farm on your left until you reach a crossroads with Rue

This may have been where Second Lieutenant Tom Garside and 18 Platoon were positioned

Wallon Cappel. Turn left and stop by the former farm buildings which have been developed into a residential complex.

This is possibly the farm building where **Second Lieutenant Tom Garside** and **18 Platoon** were positioned. Garside's platoon was on the extreme west of the town and he may have 'blotted his copybook' by asking to be withdrawn from the farm as a gunner officer had told him 'a large armoured force was heading towards him'. This was not the first occasion he had come to Captain Saunder's attention, as earlier in the campaign, at Waterloo, he refused to take a patrol through the De Coinet anti-tank fence on the grounds that it would be closed on his return. At some point in the morning of 27 May his concerns regarding the strength of German armoured vehicles appear to have got the better of him and he abandoned his post to fall back to some houses on the edge of town. He finally arrived at BHQ on Rue de la Sous-Préfécture and was taken prisoner by the Germans on 28 May.

Having turned left into Rue Wallon Cappel, continue until you have returned to the junction with Rue de Calais. Turn right here and continue for some 380 yards to the major crossroads with Rue de Sercus - which was the southern boundary between D Company and **Captain Rupert Barry's** C Company. At the crossroads go straight over for another 400 yards and turn right into Rue du Westhoek. If you continue past the new housing development to where the road narrows, the farm buildings on the left are in the approximate position of **Second Lieutenant Geoffrey Rowe's 13 Platoon**.

The 34-year-old Rowe was recommended for the award of an MC by Barry, which was eventually reduced to a Mention in Despatches. He was mortally wounded during the fighting and has no known grave. Apart from the **13 Platoon** positions, there is very little to see of the remainder of the C Company platoon

147

positions, although Barry's HQ was described by **Sergeant Phipps** as being in 'an above ground air raid shelter in the grounds of an electricity works'. This possibly places Company HQ in the electricity works on Rue du Biest – which can be found east of Rue d'Aire. By the late afternoon of 27 May the C Company positions were very hard pressed and Heyworth agreed to the company falling back to form a new line reinforced by the remaining men of A Company. It was shortly after this that Sergeant Phipps says he and Barry were cut off from the Company. All the indications suggest C Company fought on until they were overwhelmed.

After being sent to reinforce C Company, **Second Lieutenant Michael Sherwell** and the men of **7 Platoon** were positioned in houses on either side of a street, where he personally dealt with several enemy snipers before successfully leading his men south to Motte au Bois. The citation for his MC– gazetted on 20 December 1940 – hints at the chaos of battle that must have raged around the C Company positions, remarking that, 'This manoeuvre was carried out under machine gun fire and was only accomplished by the coolness and daring of 2/Lt Sherwell'.

We are now going to turn left into Rue du Boist and follow the road round past private houses to reach the major junction with Rue d'Aire. Turn left here and stop.

This is the area known as the Trocadero, where the tower of the same name once stood near Rue d'Aire. **Second Lieutenant Morton** and the men of **14 Platoon** were astride the Rue d'Aire covering the south western approaches from Morbecque - which was one of the three principle lines of attack undertaken by 8th Panzer Division. Our next stop is on Rue de Merville.

Continue along Rue d'Aire for another 600 yards - crossing over the junction with Rue de Calais and Rue de la Motte au Bois - towards the town centre. Turn right into Rue du Château de l'Orme, continuing until you reach the T-junction with Rue Pyckaert. Turn left here and keep on to the junction with Rue de Merville, turn left and stop.

The third platoon from C Company - **15 Platoon** - were positioned in houses around Rue Pyckaert. Rue de Merville was also known as the 'south east road' and was the road along which 50-year-old **Captain QM Pallet** formed a defensive line with his drivers and admin staff behind C Company after they were driven back. Pallet had been a warrant officer in the previous war and, after escaping south, along with Michael Sherwell joined the 4/Royal West Kents at Motte au Bois and led a counter-attack to push the SS out of the village. He was awarded the MC, which was gazetted in December 1940. Today, much of the Rue de Merville still consists of fabric factories and it was along here that Pallet housed the battalion transport in a 'linen factory'. Exactly which one it was is difficult to pinpoint but there are several contenders. It was at the entrance to the factory that **Private George Davies** had a close encounter with a sniper's bullet.

There are numerous factories along Rue de Merville

Continue to the roundabout and turn right onto Rue de l'Église. The church of St Eloi is on your right, where there is parking available.

The church tower is where **Second Lieutenant Palmer** controlled the artillery fire from the 98/Field Regiment Command Post at le Souverain Farm. **Second Lieutenant Keeble** and No.2 Section from 226/Field Company, Royal Engineers, based itself in St Eloi's churchyard. The spire you can see was entirely destroyed by German shellfire and not replaced until 1994.

The B Company posts under the command of **Captain John Kaye** ran along the railway line. To reach them, the shortest route lies straight on from the church along Rue de l'Église into Place du Général de Gaulle, where a left turn – following signposts to Lille, Dunkerque and St Omer – directs you to a roundabout. Following signs for the A25, turn right along Boulevard de l'Abbé Lemire to the underpass, which takes you to a roundabout. Ignoring the underpass, turn right at the roundabout along Rue de Dunkerque and Rue de la Gare to the railway station and find a parking place.

The underpass is where **10 Platoon** and **Second Lieutenant Bill Marshall** were positioned to prevent an attack via the Cité des Cheminots. This route, which ran from the north of the town, was another of the principle lines of the German attack. The station building is where **Second Lieutenant Tony Hope**

149

The underpass where 10 Platoon and Second Lieutenant Bill Marshall were positioned

and **12 Platoon** were based, while B Company HQ was in the hotel opposite the station. Finding the **11 Platoon** positions is a little more complex and the railway embankment that sheltered **Second Lieutenant Clive le Neve Foster** is best viewed from Rue du Fer á Cheval; however, a view is practically all you will get! This road takes the form of a crescent and hosts a number of industrial units.

From the station continue along Rue de la Gare and as it becomes Rue de Vieux-Berquin you will see the crescent on the left. Ignore the first turning and after taking the second, continue to the top of the crescent from where you will see the railway embankment. Return to the Rue de Vieux-Berquin and retrace your steps to Place du Général de Gaulle and park your vehicle. A short ten

B Company HQ was in the hotel opposite the station, a building which still stands today

Second Lieutenant Tony Hope and 12 Platoon were based in the railway station

minute walk from here will take you to Rue de la Sous-Préfécture via Rue de Maréchal Leclerc. At the five-way junction the reconstructed Foundation Warin Orphanage is just over 200 yards along the narrow Rue de la Sous-Préfécture.

The reconstructed **Foundation Warin Orphanage** can be found on the left side of the street. Walk on to the end of the building to the gate near the junction

The reconstructed Foundation Warin Orphanage

THE DEFENCE OF HAZEBROUCK

The Orphanage, previously on this site, was the final defensive position of the First Buckinghamshire Battalion (TA), of the Oxfordshire and Buckinghamshire Light Infantry, in May 1940. Their defence of Hazebrouck, supported by units of the Surrey and Sussex Yeomanry, of the Royal Artillery and of the Cheshire Regiment, delayed the advance of a German Armoured Division, enabling British and French troops to escape through Dunkirk and take part in the eventual liberation of Europe.

L'Orphelinat, auparavant situé sur cet endroit, était la dernière position défensive du First Buckinghamshire Battalion (TA), de l'Oxfordshire et Buckinghamshire Light Infantry, en mai 1940. Leur défense de la ville d'Hazebrouck, soutenue par les unitées du Surrey et Sussex Yeomanry, du Royal Artillery et du Cheshire Regiment, entravait l'avance d'une division blindée Allemande et ainsi permirent aux forces Britanniques et Françaises de s'échapper à Dunkerque et de participer à la libération de l'Europe.

The memorial plaque to the 1/Buckinghamshire Battalion

with Rue de la Glacière. Walk through the gate and the memorial plaque to the 1/Buckinghamshire Battalion is on the end of the building to your left. If you walk straight ahead to the small area of shrubs and trees you will be standing on the spot where the walled garden once stood. It was here that **Major Viney** and the survivors were discovered and surrendered and where Brian Heyworth and

The site of the former orphanage walled garden

many of the casualties from HQ Company were buried after the action had concluded. Part of the old garden wall can still be seen in the nearby Rue de la Glaciêre.

Return to Rue de la Sous-Préfécture and turn left to find the Instutut St Jacques on the right side of the road. The building housed GHQ and later two platoons of **Captain Richard Steven's** A Company. **Major Brian Heyworth** was killed by a sniper as he ran across the road from the Orphanage to the Instutut St Jacques, his body reportedly lying in the road for some time afterwards.

After you return to Place du Général de Gaulle there are numerous excellent cafes where a cold beer or coffee will end your tour of the Hazebrouck defences before you visit the Communal Cemetery on Rue d'Aire.

Hazebrouck Communal Cemetery
From Place du Général de Gaulle follow the D916 Rue d'Aire – signposted Béthune - past the church of St Eloi, to find the entrance to the cemetery further along the road on the right. Up until September 1917 there were several casualty clearing stations at Hazebrouck but the

The Instutut St Jacques

German shelling that took place between September 1917 and September 1918 made it unsafe for hospitals. However, in September and October 1918, No. 9

The Cross of Sacrifice at Hazebrouck Communal Cemetery

The impressive memorial arch that leads to the communal cemetery. The spire of the St Eloi Church can be seen through the archway

British Red Cross Hospital was stationed in the town. The cemetery was used again in 1940 mainly for the burial of those killed in late May 1940, during the fighting that covered the retreat of the BEF to Dunkerque. The cemetery now contains 877 Commonwealth burials of the First World War and eighty-six from the Second World War, twenty of which are unidentified.

This is a large cemetery that contains British and French casualties. The

The Château de l'Orme as it is today

The Second World War plot lies to the right of the path.

CWGC Plot lies immediately inside the entrance to the cemetery with the First World War Graves contained in the larger plot on the left of the path and the more recent Second World War plot on the right. The Cross of Sacrifice stands alone in front of a semi-circular wall with the Château de l'Orme immediately behind it; opposite the Cross of Sacrifice stands an impressive memorial archway leading to the civilian cemetery, built to honour the French casualties of the First World War.

A first glance will reveal the nature of the Second World War plot as a focal point for those men who had died of wounds or have been brought in from the surrounding area. This accounts for the high proportion of men from the 44th Division who were involved in the fighting to the south and north east of Hazebrouck. There twenty-eight identified men of the 1/Bucks buried here, twenty-five being probable casualties of the Hazebrouck fighting. Amongst these are 33-year-old **Major Brian Kay Heyworth** (4.B.20), 21-year-old **Second Lieutenant Martin Samsome Preston** (4.B.14), who was the nephew of Robert Graves, and 32-year-old **Captain James Makepeace Ritchie** (4.B.24). Richie was a student at Wellington College before he went up to Trinity College, Oxford in 1926. He then became a Chartered Accountant and Assistant Secretary to the Banker's Clearing House Committee. He joined the Inns of Court Regiment

155

in London before transferring to the Buckinghamshire Battalion. From 98/Field Regiment there are three further casualties, including 22-year-old **Lance Sergeant Godfrey Woolven** and 21-year-old **Gunner Daniel O'Donnell,** who were killed manning the 392/Battery gun at les Cinq Rues.

The First World War Plot contains a large number of men who died of wounds in the various field hospitals. One of these was 40-year-old **Lieutenant Colonel Derrick Carden** (II.B.10.) who was educated at Wellington College and was commanding the 1/7 Argyll and Sutherland Highlanders when he was mortally wounded in May 1915. **Lieutenant Colonel Clarence Daly** (III.R.24.) was commanding the 6/Battalion of the Australian Imperial Force when he was killed in the Fôret de Nieppe in April 1918. Another officer who died of wounds was 29-year-old **Lieutenant Cecil Gilliat** (II.D.39.). Gilliat died of his wounds on 13 October 1914 whilst serving with the 1/Royal Warwicks at Meteren. His twin brother, Reginald, served as a Captain in the the Leinster Regiment and was killed on 6 April 1915 and is buried at Rue-du-Bacquerot No.1 Military Cemetery, Laventie. Cecil Gilliat's posthumous promotion to captain appeared in the same issue of the *London Gazette* that announced that a certain Lieutenant B L Montgomery had been promoted to captain. You will also find Canadian born **Driver Benjamin de Fer** (I.A.18.), who was executed for the murder of **RSM James Scott** (I.A.10.) in August 1918 and **Private Avon Roderique** (III.C.35), who murdered the two officers you may have already visited in the Hondeghem Churchyard Cemetery. The two non-standard headstones belong to **Lieutenant Thomas Elliot** (II.G.20), who was killed serving with the 1/Northumberland Brigade, RFA, in October 1915, and London born **Private Reginald Walker** (I.B.22.), who died of wounds two days before Christmas in 1916.

Selected Bibliography

The National Archives

Unit War Diaries in WO 166 and 167.

Personal accounts in CAB 106 and WO 217.

POW Reports in WO 344, WO 373.

Imperial War Museum Sound Archive

King's College Archive

The National Army Museum

The RUSI Library

SOFO Archive

Published Sources

Blaxland, G, *Destination Dunkirk: The Story of Gort's Army*, William Kimber 1973.

Brooks, G, *Grand Party*, Hutchinson 1942.

Butler, E, *Mason-Mac*, Macmillan 1972.

Daniell, D S, *Cap of Honour*, White Lion 1951.

Duncan, M, *Underground from Posen*, William Kimber 1954.

Ellis, L, *The War in France and Flanders*, HMSO 1953.

Ellis, F, *The Welsh Guards at War*, London Stamp Exchange 1989.

Heyworth, M, *Hazebrouck 1940*, privately published 2000.

Jackson, J, *The Fall of France,* OUP 2003.

Neville, M C, *The Ox and Bucks Light Infantry Chronicle Vol 1*, Gale and Polden 1949.

Mace, P, *Forrard*, Leo Cooper 2001.

McNab, R, *Retreat from Riviere*, Digital Print Media 2013.

Messiant, J, *L'Occupation a Cassel (1940-1945),* privately published 2011.

Murland, J D, *Retreat and Rearguard: Dunkirk 1940*, Pen and Sword 2015.

Philson, A, *The British Army 1939-1945 Organization and order of Battle Volume 6*, Military Press 2007.

Sebag-Montefiore, H, *Dunkirk – Fight to the Last Man*, Viking 2006.

Summer, I and Wilson, R, *Yeomanry of the East Riding*, Hutton 1993.

Wild, D, *Prisoner of Hope*, The Book Guild 1992.

Williams, D, *The New Contemptibles*, John Murray 1940.

Appendix

Notes on some of the individuals mentioned in the text

Name	Evacuated	PoW	KiA or DoW	Cemetery	Decoration
100/Field Company Royal Engineers					
Maj G Whitehead		yes			MiD
Capt W Deacon		yes			
Lt J Mercer		yes			
Driver J Ware			yes	Oudezeele Churchyard	
Spr L Davies			yes	Dunkirk Memorial	
226/Field Company Royal Engineers					
2/Lt D Keeble	yes				
Major L J Griffith		yes			
145 Brigade Staff					
Brig N Somerset **		yes			OBE (Mil)
Capt H Lovett	yes				MiD
2/Gloucesters					
Lt Col M Gilmore		yes			DSO
Major C R Campbell		yes			
Capt E Jones		yes			
2/Lt G French			yes	Cassel Communal	
Capt QM R Brasington	yes				MC
Lt I O Spencer RAMC		yes			MiD
Sgt I Kibble		yes			
Major W Percy-Hardman		yes			MC
Pte A Tickner		yes			MiD
CSM P 'Dodger' Brown		yes			
Pte H Vaughan	yes				
Sgt H Gallagher*		yes			
2/Lt R Cresswell		yes			MC
L/Cpl D Ruddy			yes	Longuenesse Souvenir	
PSM B Oxtoby **		yes	Repatriated 1944		MM/MBE
Sgt A Nix		yes			

Name	Evacuated	PoW	KiA or DoW	Cemetery	Decoration
Capt H C Wilson		yes			MiD
Lt R Olive			yes	Dunkirk Memorial	
2/Lt J Fane	yes				MC
L/Cpl J Eldridge	yes				
Sig A Smythe	yes				
CQMS E Farmer			yes	Dunkirk Memorial	
L/Cpl P Badnell			yes	Dunkirk Memorial	
Sgt G White		yes			
Pte W Phelps			yes	Dunkirk Memorial	
Pte A Palmer			yes		
L/Cpl F Greenhough	yes				
L/Cpl J Eldridge	yes				
PSM E Morgan			yes	Helfaut Churchyard	
2/Lt G Weightman			yes	Cassel Communal	
Capt E Lynn-Allen		yes			MC
2/Lt T Reeve-Tucker*		yes			MiD
Lt N Rice		yes			
Capt A Cholmondeley		yes	Held at Colditz Castle		
CSM F Robinson		yes			
PSM W Rumble			yes	Cassel Communal	
4/Oxfordshire and Buckinghamshire Light Infantry					
Rev D Wild		yes			MC
Lt/Col G Kennedy		yes			DSO
Maj J Thorne			yes	Cassel Communal	MiD
Maj G Wykeham			yes	Oye-Plage Communal	
Capt M Fleming			yes	Lille Southern	MiD
Capt L Falkiner			yes	Oye-Plage Communal	
2/Lt P Pearman-Smith			yes	Kortrijk St Jan	
Lt E Keen		yes			MiD
2/Lt J Clerke Brown			yes	Longuenesse Souvenir	
2/Lt N Ruck Nightingale			yes	Dunkirk Memorial	
Maj J Graham			yes	Dunkirk Memorial	
Lt M Duncan **		yes	Escaped from Posen in Sept 1941		MC
2/Lt C Dilwyn			yes	Oye-Plage Communal	
Capt N Lansdell RAMC		yes			MiD
Capt C Rathcreedan		yes			
Capt C Clutsom		yes			MiD

Name	Evacuated	PoW	KiA or DoW	Cemetery	Decoration
CSM C Bailey DCM			yes	Nine Elms British Cem	
1/Buckinghamshire Battalion – Oxford and Buckinghamshire Light Infantry					
Maj B Heyworth			yes	Hazebrouck Communal	MiD
Maj E Viney		yes			DSO
Capt J Richie			yes	Hazebrouck Communal	
2/Lt D Stebbings		yes			MC
Capt QM C Pallet	yes				MC
Capt B Mason	yes				
Lt T Gibbens RAMC **		yes			MBE (Mil)
RSM A Hawtin		yes	Escaped from Thorn in Jan 1944		MiD
Capt B Dowling		yes			MiD
2/Lt M Preston			yes	Hazebrouck Communal	
2/Lt J Viccars		yes			MiD
Capt R Stevens	yes				
2/Lt W Nelson		yes			MiD
2/Lt M Sherwell	yes				MC
Capt J Kaye	yes				
2/Lt C Le Neve Foster	yes				MiD
2/Lt J Hope	yes				
2/Lt W Marshall	yes				
2/Lt T Garside		yes			
2/Lt A Lee	yes				
2/Lt G Rowe			yes	Dunkirk Memorial	MiD
2/Lt L Powell		yes			
Capt H Saunders	yes				
Capt R Barry **		yes	Held at Colditz Castle		MBE(Mil)
Sgt L Phipps		yes			MM
2/Lt L Powell		yes			MiD
CSM L Badrick		yes			
Sgt R Print		yes			
Cpl S Abbot		yes			
Cpl B Youens		yes			
4/Cheshires					
Maj Gore-Hickman			yes	Brugge General Cemetery	

Name	Evacuated	PoW	KiA or DoW	Cemetery	Decoration
2/Lt F Golland			yes	Hotton War Cemetery	
Pte M Reynolds	yes				
140/Field Company – 362 Battery					
Lt Col C Odling		yes			
Maj E Milton			yes	Longuenesse Souvenir	
Maj C Christopherson		yes			MiD
Capt D Lacey RAMC		yes			MiD
Lt C Bennett	yes				
Lt R Baxter		yes			
Lt J May	yes		yes	Bromley Hill (UK)	
Sgt H Swindle			yes	Dunkirk Memorial	
Driver W Martin **		yes	Escaped August 1940		DCM
145 Brigade Anti-Tank Company					
2/Lt D Wallis	yes		KiA Arnhem 1944, Oosterbeek War Cem		MiD
Lt J C Robertson		yes			
Capt E Dixie			yes	Cassel Communal	
Pte G Blake			yes	Bavinchove Church-yard	
Sgt K Trussell		yes			DCM
209 & 211 Battery 53/Anti-Tank Regiment					
Maj R Cartland			yes	Hotton War Cemetery	
Lt H Freeker		yes			
Maj H Mercer		yes			MiD
2/Lt R Hutton-Squire			yes	Proven Churchyard	
Bomdr H Munn		yes			
Pte F Barber		yes			
143/Field Ambulance					
Major J G Lawson **		yes			MiD/MBE
1/Light Armoured Reconnaissance Brigade – 1/ERY and 1/Fife and Forfar Yeomanry					
Brig C Norman	yes				
Lt Col R Sharp			yes	Warhem Communal	
Sgt C Lloyd			yes	Bavinchove Church-yard	
Lt Col W Thompson		yes			MiD
Maj G Radcliffe			yes	Hotton War Cemetery	
Maj H Wright		yes			DSO
Capt D Hall			yes	Hotton War Cemetery	
2/Lt N Wilmot-Smith		yes			MC
2/Lt M Lindley		yes			

162

Name	Evacuated	PoW	KiA or DoW	Cemetery	Decoration
2/Lt N Bonner		yes			
2/Lt J Cockin			yes	Hotton War Cemetery	
2/Lt J Dixon		yes			
Cpl H Parnaby		yes			
Cpl T Rowe		yes			
Cpl H Moore	yes				
Trooper C Dodsworth		yes			
Trooper H Ostler			yes	St-Sylvestre -Cappel	
Trooper W Ostler			yes	Hotton War Cemetery	
TSM T Arbon			yes	St-Sylvestre -Cappel	
5/RHA					
Major R Hoare	yes				DSO
Capt B Teacher	yes				MC
BSM R Millard	yes				DCM
2/Lt M Lanyon	yes				
Gunner R Manning			yes	Longuenesse Souvenir	
TSM R Ophie		yes			
Gunner C Kavanagh	yes				MM
98/Field Regiment					
Lt Col G Ledingham	yes				DSO
L/Sgt G Woolven			yes	Hazebrouck Communal	
Sgt J Mordin	yes				DCM
Maj C Egerton			yes	Terlincthun British	
Maj Hon C Cubitt	yes				MiD
Capt Lord Cowdray	yes				
2/Lt J Palmer	yes				MC
Gunner R Scoates			yes	Steenwerck Communal	
223/Battery 56/Anti-Tank Regiment					
Maj I C Pedley	yes				
2/Lt D Timms	yes				
German Army Personnel – ranks shown as in May 1940					
General der Panzertruppen Heinz Guderian			Held in US custody until 1948. Died 1954		
General der Panzertruppen Werner Kempf			Released from custody in 1947. Died 1964		
Oberstleutnant Richard Koll			Released from custody in 1946. Died 1963		
Oberst Hans-Karl von Esebeck			Sympathetic to the anti-Hitler conspiracy, arrested in 1944. Died 1955		
Oberst Johann von Ravenstein			Captured near Tobruk in 1941. Died 1962		

Hauptmann Eric Löwe	KiA near Losovka, Russia, in 1943
Leutnant Kelletat	Survived the war, date of death unknown
Generalleutnant Georg-Hans Reinhardt	Successfully prosecuted for war crimes. Died 1963
Generalleutnant Adolph-Friedrich Kuntzen	Retired 1944. Died 1964
Oberst Walter Neumann-Silkow	DoW in Libya 1941
Oberstleutnant Friedrich Sieberg	DoW near Krivoi Rog 1943
Oberstleutnant Karl-Adolph von Bodecker	Released from captivity March 1946. Died 1983
Oberstleutnant Wilhelm Cristolli	KiA in Italy 1944
Generalleutnant der Waffen SS Paul Hausser	Wrote *Waffen SS in Action* in 1953. Died 1972

*Fought with the 1/Gloucesters on the Imjin River, Korea, in April 1951
** Award made for either escaping captivity or as a result of activity as a POW. Where there are two awards shown, the first is usually for actions during or after the defence of Cassel/Hazebrouck and the second is for conduct whilst a POW.

Index